Falling in Love...
(with the camera)

LIFE LESSONS ON PRESENTATION IMPROVEMENT
FROM A HOLLYWOOD ACTOR AND A CPA

Facing your fears to create knockout professional videos
while unleashing your AUTHENTIC SELF!

Kate Zenna and David Wolfe

Published by BookLocker.com, Inc., Bradenton, Florida.

Printed on acid-free paper.

Booklocker.com, Inc.
2017

First Edition

DISCLAIMER

This book details the authors' personal experiences with and opinions about marketing and business.

The authors and publisher are providing this book and its contents, on an "as is" basis and make no representations or warranties of any kind with respect to this book or its contents. The author and publisher disclaim all such representations and warranties, including for example warranties of merchantability and consulting advice for a particular purpose. In addition, the authors and publisher do not represent or warrant that the information accessible via this book is accurate, complete, or current.

The statements made about products or services have not been evaluated by the U.S. government. Please consult with your own legal professional regarding the suggestions and recommendations made in this book.

Except as specifically stated in this book, neither the authors nor publisher, not any authors, contributors, or other representatives will be liable for damages arising out of, or in connection with, the use of this book. This is a comprehensive limitation of liability that applies to all damages of any kind, including (without limitation) compensatory; direct, indirect or consequential damages; loss of data, income or profit; loss of or damage to property and claims of third parties.

You understand that this book is not intended as a substitute for consultation with a licensed medical, legal, or accounting professional. Before you begin any change to your lifestyle in any way, you will consult a licensed professional to ensure that you are doing what's best for your situation.

This book provides content related to marketing and business topics. As such, use of this book implies your acceptance of this disclaimer.

Praise for <u>Falling in Love... (with the camera)</u>

"Having worked with Kate Zenna during the filming of our family legacy movie I can personally attest to what David and Kate have written in their new book. Kate has the ability to just know what needs to be done to bring out the best of somebody on camera. My four brothers and I are very different people. Kate was a chameleon who changed to the unique needs of each of us. She is funny, insightful, and a consummate professional.

If you are nervous about appearing on video I would recommend two things: one, buy this book and two, hire ZennaWolfe to help you through the process. They handle all of the heavy lifting and they are a lot of fun to boot."

Alison Winter
CEO – Braintree Holdings, LLC
CEO – Gracious Exit

"I have had the pleasure of both reading this terrific book by Kate and David, AND of working with them in the studio to create a video business card for my mortgage loan business. Everything that Kate talks about in the book is true – she used the exact same techniques and strategies when I was in the studio with her. I came in a little tentative and my first few takes showed this. Then Kate Zenna stepped in and brought me out of my shell. She has a great technique in getting somebody to relax in front of the camera and to just, well, have a conversation with her as if we were sitting in a coffee shop. I wished I would have had this book to read before I met with ZennaWolfe team last year. In the book David talks about there being some 'bravery' involved in agreeing to come into the studio. I agree

with him – I had to think about whether I wanted to come in before I agreed to do it. I am so glad I did! Kudos to Kate and David. This is a good and an important book."

Calvin Jones
Mortgage Loan Professional

"Kate and David are consummate professionals with the added bonus of being exceptionally wonderful and talented people. I have worked with them both in and out of the studio and have learned so much witnessing the way they do business. This book is rich with wonderful advice about how to work on camera but it also comes with so many incredible insights about living at your highest level, which in turns makes on-camera appearances so much better!

I love their two distinct voices in the book and how both Kate and David share their personal stories of discovering how to perform consistently at the extraordinary levels that they do. Their journeys to this place have been so vastly different and yet there is a common theme in their wisdom about learning to live authentically and trusting that you know what you are doing. We all need these reminders! No matter who you are or what you do, you will benefit from reading this book, and maybe the next time a camera is pointed your way, you can look down the barrel of the lens with confidence. This book will help you do just that!"

Kathryn Winslow
Actor

"I had a fantastic experience, and it was a lot more fun than I ever anticipated. It was interesting and I learned a lot. To be honest, I was sort of dreading it before I arrived for the sessions, but afterwards, I'm just so glad I was there. It was comforting having Kate out there interviewing us and asking the questions and smiling at us – just giving us that positive energy. I just can't imagine that we didn't improve and feel more comfortable in front of the camera. I would definitely recommend this program. I think that it's not only a good experience but it's also a lot of fun, and I feel like I got to know my colleagues a lot better. I got to know them on a different level, which has been very rewarding.

My big takeaway is that when you're in front of a camera, you feel compelled to speak; but it's okay to pause, collect your thoughts, smile, and let the camera wait. I felt like the moment I walked into the building that someone has been doting over me, feeding me, bringing me coffee, fixing my hair and makeup, and encouraging me. It can be very difficult to speak publicly or in front of a camera and any time somebody can get training or additional assistance in that area, I think that makes them a better presenter in front of their clients and prospects.

I wasn't sure what to expect, but it is a very polished and professional outfit. You come in and there are cameras and people everywhere and you truly do feel like you're on a movie set. I didn't really expect that. In fact, my makeup session – I thought they would put some powder on my nose, hand me a script, and move me into a room – which was not what it was at all. Again, it was very polished and professional."

Terry Donaldson
Real Estate Professional

"I've had the pleasure of working with Kate and David on most of their productions. I can flat out say that this book is a testament to how they go about their business both in and out of the studio. David runs things outside of the studio where Kate is the CEO once inside the studio walls. Time and time again I have seen her work her magic with clients. They come in nervous and unsure and then there is this transformation that occurs because of her unique ability to laser focus on a person's fear spot and to address it – usually through humor and always with a lot of loving support. It's so great that they have created this book and if you look closely you will see that

David has included tidbits of marketing and business mentorship for the reader as well. I would definitely consider David one of my great business mentors and have grown from sitting in on his business 'lessons' while in meetings with him at his office. He took time to listen to my production input as well as ideas and helped me focus my own goals with building a business. Those of us pursuing big creative and business oriented goals - are lucky to have a Kate and David on our side! The results are winning!

Run, don't walk, and buy this book. And once you do think about booking a day in the studio with them. You will not be sorry – in fact it could be a life-changing event for you as it has been for other ZennaWolfe clients."

Audrey Henry
Actor and Photographer

"We wanted to have a family video that would tell the story of our family with memories from all the surviving siblings. We

wanted to capture our stories while we still could and create a treasured memory for our children and the generation after that and the generation after that. ZennaWolfe saw the value of that and saw a way to make that happen, and, basically, Hollywood came to my sister's house and they set up lights and boom mics and cameras in multiple locations. In a couple of days, they captured a lifetime of stories, and it was an awesome experience.

I would totally recommend this to anyone who wants to have a treasured keepsake for their family or give a gift of memories to someone in their family. It's an amazing, amazing opportunity that ZennaWolfe made happen. The professionalism of all the staff is something I'll remember – I have a production background so I can appreciate how personable and patient they were. They didn't get annoyed with me asking questions and they appreciated having someone around that could understand a little of what was going on. That's what I'm going to remember: an opportunity to see how the pros work.

Kate was so approachable and she has a great ability to get different takes on our stories from all the siblings and weave them together to create one unified story. David did a great job overseeing the production. The amount of coordination that was involved in this and the amount of attention to detail is very difficult – I know because I do this for a living. And, it is really incredible the level of professionalism and the level of detail they keep track of. Kudos to both David and Kate."

Jim Adams
Professional Videographer

"Terror and Dread pretty much sum up how I felt before my studio session with Kate. In front of a camera, I typically get nervous and freeze up, forgetting what I'm supposed to say. Fortunately, this experience was nothing like how I pictured it to be!! I was surprised at how natural the coaching process felt. By the end of my session, it was like I was just having a conversation with someone and was no longer distracted by the camera facing me. And on playback, I was shocked at how relaxed I looked on camera, and how it really looked like me. Not some nervous, weird version of myself.

Little did I know that I would immediately notice other "benefits" in my everyday work. I found that leading calls/meetings, presenting and answering impromptu questions in a group was easier. I'm much better at it now. Kate taught me to host the party. Changing my mindset to being a good host has transformed how I lead or present. People seem to actually WANT to participate! Talk about a confidence booster. I've learned to embrace the "pause" instead of filling silence with annoying or awkward words. I use the pause to my advantage now. These are just a couple of examples of what this experience has done for me. Bottom line, this is powerful, transformative stuff!! If an introvert like me can see the difference, you can too!"

Amy Beesley
Technology Consultant

"My day in the studio was amazing. I liked the team building aspect – it was great to be together with a group of my colleagues. And it was a new experience. I think we gained a

couple of tricks, tips and techniques, and I'll definitely remember to host the party.

What I took away from the session is that we all say "um", "uh" and "you know" too much and, instead, it's better to have some pauses. Your audience doesn't know what you're thinking, so you can have a short pause and an inflection point, which doesn't have to be a bad thing. The other thing I took away is "hosting the party", which means – if you're speaking – it's your show and your audience should feel comfortable like they would at any gathering at your house."

Greg Roberts
Software Professional

"I am incredibly excited to be writing a testimonial for Kate and David's book because I am in the midst of shooting both a video business card and informational videos with them right now. What I find beautiful now is working closely with Kate in prepping, structuring, and shooting my videos. For me, the process was a little like unpeeling an orange. Initially my approach was direct and succinct, the way I would handle a business deal.

What Kate did was take my ideology and thoughts - promoted a lot of back-and-forth communication – which enabled me to anticipate the succulent fruit of the creative interaction. Together we laid the foundation so that when I sat in front of the camera - she and I discussed the content in my own words – I became familiar and completely comfortable with what I had to say. During thirty-plus years in the corporate media world I was involved in writing plans, presentations, and sat through hundreds of brain storming sessions during which structure needed to be set and then acted upon. I can honestly say I can count on one hand how many times we were successful. Kate gathered information, brain-stormed, set structure, and got me where I needed to be quickly and easily. I felt invigorated, satisfied, and confident! I can't imagine using another company to shoot my videos. They brought out the true me and who could ask for anything more!"

Susan Sanford
Real Estate Agent

Acknowledgments

Special thanks to Maggie Wolfe who, while managing to extricate herself from working with David on his videos, did yeoman's work in the evenings and weekends proofing this manuscript and working with the publisher to insure its completion. Thanks, Puppy.

We have been blessed to have such amazing crews at our Los Angeles and Dallas studios. To our productions crews, thank you so much for your trust in us in the beginning and your patience in our rookie-ness. Two people in particular deserve special mention: Audrey Henry (who took all of the photographs for the book) and Robert Murphy. Both of these special people are very active in the entertainment business but can be counted upon to move mountains to work on our projects. They are family to both of us.

There are many people who have helped us in setting ZennaWolfe on such an unbelievable trajectory from the get-go. But the credit goes to the Brave Ones. Our clients. These strong and terrific people who had the bravery to put their trust in ZennaWolfe. You know who you are and we thank you.

Kate Zenna Acting Credits

With over twenty major film and television credits to her name, Kate Zenna has established herself as a versatile and noteworthy actor in both the American and Canadian entertainment markets. During her coaching sessions of non-professional on-camera talent, Kate draws upon the experience she gained while shooting 40+ episodes of network television series and numerous films and TV movies. Her work opposite many world class movie and television stars has deeply influenced how she works with private clients and how she leads the ship at ZennaWolfe Media. Some of the stars she's played opposite include: Timothy Hutton, Susan Sarandon, William Hurt, Matthew Modine, Rob Lowe, Rob Morrow, Mena Suvari, Annabeth Gish, Jon Stamos, Balthazar Getty, Calista Flockhart and Garry Marshall.

Here is a partial list of Kate's acting credits:

Films and TV Movies

Sex and Lies in Sin City (Lifetime), Director Peter Medak
Ramona and Beezus (Fox 2000), Director Elizabeth Allen
Soldier's Girl (Showtime), Director Frank Pierson
Ice Bound (CBS)
Master Spy: The Robert Hanssen Story (CBS), Director Lawrence Schiller
Love is Work, Director Johnny Kalangis
Chicago (Miramax), Director Rob Marshall
Sealed with a Kiss (CBS), Director Ron Lagomarsino
Jack and Jill (Alliance Atlantis), Director Johnny Kalangis

Television

The Fosters (ABC Family)
Extant (CBS)
Port Hope (CBC)
I'm in the Band (Disney XD)
Eleventh Hour (CBS)
Brothers and Sisters (ABC)
Queer as Folk (Showtime)
Puppets Who Kill (Comedy Network)
Train 46 (Global)
Zoe Busiek: Wild Card (Lifetime)
Street Time (Showtime)
A Nero Wolfe Mystery (A&E)
Twice in a Lifetime (PAX)

Books by David Wolfe

Software and Vendors and Requirements, Oh My! – A Project Team's Guide to Evaluating Business Software

Lessons From the Technology Front Line: Out of The Trenches Advice from a real estate software mercenary to help take the fear and risk out of your migration from one major software platform to another

Marching to the Beat of a Different Drummer - Lessons Learned During a Professional Life (and discovering the business I was REALLY in along the way...)

Out Front: Business Building Strategies from Frontline Entrepreneurs (Contributor)

Contents

Introduction
By David Wolfe

My story begins in October 2007. I attended a marketing conference in Tampa Bay and one of the many lessons I took away from that conference was the notion that if you were the Founder or President of a company, then you needed to be the focus of all of the marketing and sales efforts. I was told I should be writing books, being interviewed, and being the centerpiece of our website...and I should be making videos. I had been studying a really, really good marketer and attorney named Ben Glass who used videos on his website to give away free important information to prospects who were interested in understanding their rights if they were involved in a car accident. (In most states lawyers cannot advertise but there is nothing that said they couldn't give away information and show their expertise. Smart.) I liked that tactic for my software consulting firm, Lupine Partners. There is a lot of fear and anxiety that goes with a software migration and I saw this type of educational video as an excellent opportunity to dip my toe into the video-making waters.

And so it began...little did I know of the frustration and humiliation to come. Nor did I have any idea that I would meet my future business partner because of this decision. And I certainly didn't know that Kate and I would create a company that specialized in on-camera performance. Or that I would become a Producer on film projects for a myriad of clients working hand-in-hand with Kate on set. Me?

I started my software consulting firm Lupine Partners in 1993. Thinking back, I didn't even know what marketing was. I certainly had no strategy around obtaining clients. I just sat around and waited for the phone to ring – which fortunately it did for quite a number of years. Until it didn't anymore – thus the need to attend the Tampa Bay conference. My sixth sense told me I was going to go out of business unless I took matters into my own hands.

I must say I was not particularly looking forward to making these educational videos. I didn't start working on the videos until about six weeks after the Tampa Bay conference. I remember it was between Christmas and New Year's. I was two months away from turning 50 years old. The anxiety I felt was around how I would be perceived by others – particularly my competitors. As I sit here and write this I am just shaking my head. Man, I have come a long way. I couldn't give a damn now what they think about me. Truly. But back then, for some reason, it was a big concern for me. And then there were friends and family. I didn't know it then (and still didn't know it until Kate knocked some sense into me years later), but I was also unwittingly pulling myself down to be like other people. Not being my authentic self – and part of my authentic self is 'going for it'. I had some childhood belief issues around 'not getting above your raising'. Not getting too big for your britches type of mindset. Before I even sat down in front of the camera, I had all sorts of issues that I didn't even know I had.

So, I went out and purchased a video camera. A nice one. And a tripod. Didn't think about sound. (Who knew?). It was finally the night to record my videos. What to wear? Well, a coat and tie of course. Know this – I NEVER wear a tie. Never. Good call, Wolfe – let's go create videos that go out into the world with you being as inauthentic as you possibly could be. This was the first of many, many mistakes I would make in front of a camera. And the mistake was this: Trying to be what I thought people expected me to be rather than being who I am.

I set up the camera on the tripod. Just me. Didn't need any help. How hard could all of this be? Back and forth I would go. Sitting down and then getting up to look in the camera viewfinder. Problem: I couldn't see myself in the viewfinder because I was behind the viewfinder. It never occurred to me that it's, at minimum, a two-person job. So, I would use my remote control to record myself for a few brief seconds to make sure I was positioned correctly. Finally – had it just right. Time for my first take! (I was CERTAIN I would be able to do all of my videos in one take. I read that's how Frank Sinatra did it when he was filming The Manchurian Candidate in the early 1960's. How hard could this be?)

Ready… Action! "Hi, I'm David Wolfe………………" Complete and utter silence. F-word! It felt like the room was getting warmer. I got up and went and played back that three seconds of video so I could watch myself. Horrors. I looked like I was being held captive (more on the 'Taliban' videos later in the book). Okay – that was an anomaly. Let's jump back on that saddle. Second and third take were exactly the same. Beyond knowing my name and starting with a greeting (deciding that 'hello' was better than 'hi'), I had nothing. Nada. Zip. Complete and utter choke artist. I actually talk to people all day long. I'm good at it. Witty. Considered profound by some. Deep. But this plastic box was really kicking my ass!

By the fifth take I got beyond my name, rank, and serial number. Who knows what I said – but I do remember what I felt and that was the dripping of sweat down my back and under my arms. (Uh, wearing a coat and tie…) I decided to call it a night. I went and took the camera off the stupid tripod and took everything upstairs to the office closet.

I didn't try again for six months.

If you are reading this book, and even though I don't know who you are you are, I know this: You are probably similar to me. I am not an actor. You aren't either…probably. My guess is you have a tale of woe around making presentations or standing on stage in front of a bunch of people, or maybe even 'going around the room' and introducing yourself. I'll bet you are not crazy about being in front of a camera – and I'll bet if you do happen to get captured on video that you don't come across like your 'normal self' or that you are happy with your appearance.

Well, that's how I was until the powers that be had decided that they had had enough of my nonsense and decided to introduce Kate Zenna to me. Of the many good and wonderful things that have come from our partnership, the first and the biggest was her ability to clean up my act in front of the camera. And it didn't take that long – just a few nips and tucks during a day of filming.

If she can fix me, then she and her posse of working actors can fix you. And that's why we have written this book together. To fix the other David Wolfe's out there. I'm hoping this book will change your life like Kate changed mine. Or at a minimum, give you the confidence and the tools to begin filming yourself.

Maybe even teach you how to fall in love… (with the camera).

Part I
Why All of This is Important

"To be yourself in a world that is constantly trying to make you something else is the greatest accomplishment."

Ralph Waldo Emerson

Chapter 1
The World Has Changed

By David Wolfe

The business world HAS changed – I don't know if you have noticed that fact or not.

In the 'old' world people made phone calls and had lunch meetings (in person!) to discuss business. The idea of creating a video for business reasons and (horrors!) putting that same video on the internet was not something a reputable, savvy professional would ever do.

The NEW world is a texting and video world. Apparently, with the exception of me (and you!), nobody seems to read a book any more. Increasingly people get their information by watching short videos. And it's not like this phenomenon is in process – it has fully arrived. It used to be that you gained authority by becoming a published author. That still works but having a collection of business videos is just as valuable in getting you 'street cred'.

But there's a downside to videos - a majority of them are poorly produced and the 'star' of the videos does not come across authentically. There is usually something that is not quite right. You can't put your finger on it but something doesn't feel right. I can tell you what that something is: *inauthenticity*. It's the same feeling you get when you meet somebody who doesn't quite feel on the up and up. You don't know why you feel that way, but you just know something's off.

If you haven't been in front of a camera, you will be. And unless you are from another planet, or are Robert Duvall or Jon Voight, it is going to feel odd, uncomfortable, and unnatural. Because there is nothing natural about talking to a piece of plastic that gives no feedback at all.

But let's just say for the sake of argument that you won't be in front of a camera. Ok, that's a possibility...But you do talk to people, right? Do you have any idea how you come across during a meeting? Or a presentation? Or just one-on-one? How many times do you say "You know", "I mean", or "ummmm"? Do you make a face when you are thinking? Do you look up? Do your eyes light up when you talk? How's your energy level? Is your voice tight and trailing into oblivion? What tics do you have? Oh, you have them, trust me. You just don't know that you have them because you have not given yourself the gift, the permission, to be on camera.

Here's the deal. However bad you look on camera (or how badly you come across in real life), it's fixable and I'm walking proof of that. (More on my story in Chapters 7-9). In this book, Kate and I are going to show you what being authentic means. And your tool for learning is going to be a camera, because as the saying goes: The camera never lies. And you know what? It doesn't.

ZennaLude™

VIDEO IS BIG! HUGE! Like the push button phone, it's here to stay and it will only continue to evolve. Now apps, toys, and platforms seem to pop up daily to allow everyone to be a video star. Most of my professional friends not in the film business have been bracing themselves and I know quite a few are making like ostriches and hoping it all goes back to 1955. It's more than a cultural shift that has occurred. The world has changed forever. We now pack more informational intake into each minute of our day than we ever have before. We're busy and we need to get seven things done in one minute. I get it. It's just a fact of life now. So, if you can convince a busy person to 'go with you' or your firm in less than a minute by getting a great video in front of them, it's a win-win-WIN. You've saved everyone time. You've also saved a bunch of time if after watching your video they can tell that you're not a good personality fit for them. Phew, right?! Because guess what…they ain't for you either! We are all looking for great clients, and part of that means they need to like us just as we must like them. Video handles that first introduction for both client and professional – and you need to make sure that on video it's really YOU, not some weird, nervous version of yourself!

Chapter 2
Why You Must Be GOOD on Camera

By David Wolfe

Ok, maybe this isn't the right question. Maybe I should have used the word *authentic* instead of *good*. So, why must you be authentic on camera? Because it's YOU and you are amazing. You're not this artificial person we all put out there. I look at my old videos back from 2008 and I (and Kate) ask, "Who is THAT David Wolfe?" Yes, it's me but it's not really ME, because I hadn't been coached on how to be myself in front of the camera. I hadn't yet received tips on *Hosting the Party* (Chapter 21). Or *Taking the Pause* (Chapter 23). Or that the *Perfection is in the Imperfection* (Chapter 24).

I now take these tips from Kate to every meeting, presentation, and sales call that I make. I have fused these tips into my soul and, in doing so, have made most of Kate's tips and tactics a *habit*. Now if you are with me in a professional environment, then you are at the David Wolfe Party. Even if we are in YOUR office or conference room. This is what being good on camera teaches you. To be yourself and to share your talents with the world. Sharing the *real* you - not this make-believe person that all of us put out there on occasion.

◊ ◊ ◊ ◊ ◊ ◊ ◊ ◊ ◊

ZennaLude™

MAKE THE CONNECTION. For a long time, I was curious about what made someone good on-camera. What did 'good' even mean? I eventually realized that what I meant was compelling, interesting, and watchable. How were some people able to draw you in, to command your attention, make you care about what they were speaking about? It wasn't about being pretty or handsome or famous or rich – I had quickly deduced that. And it didn't even matter if their message was ludicrous or important.

Eventually, I determined that the people who drew ME in, on AND off-camera were people who were enthusiastically and unabashedly themselves while also being connected to the present moment with passion, enthusiasm, conviction, and authority. It didn't mean they had to be super happy or smiley or jolly or even clever in their thinking. But they were passionately connected to their message or opinion and also to the person or people with whom they were attempting to share their ideas.

This is what I focus on when working with people. Because sometimes the people I work with have lost their 'connection' to why they do what they do. It's about the money now and they are creating a video to increase business. They've forgotten that they experience great fulfillment when their services solve a customer's or client's problem. It feels good to know you are changing lives in a positive way or serving others. Keying in to that is one guaranteed way to get some sparkle from any eye!

Chapter 3
Straight Business Talk

By David Wolfe

We've all met phony people. You don't even know why they don't seem *real*, but you feel it when you see it. Being yourself is the key to being liked. Robert Cialdini found that being liked was one of the six persuasive principles of his hallmark study *Influence: The Psychology of Persuasion*. People want to buy from people they like or with whom they have affinity. This notion of authenticity is the hallmark of our work at ZennaWolfe. Our actor-coaches are also referred to as 'authenticity coaches' because they have been trained to help our clients stop being inauthentic on camera. After we are done with our clients, we see an amazing transformation. We see the reveal of the real person appear on-camera and then on their company's website. Now they have a chance to be liked. To sell. To inspire trust. To be an authority. To be a new friend. Remember that people buy because of people and they want to know who that real person is.

Prospective clients care more about knowing about you than about the services that all of us offer. This is more than just taking the prospect out to lunch or dinner. It's about you removing the mask and showing yourself to your soon-to-be client so they have a sense and measure of you. Speaking honestly about failures you may have had. Looking them in the eye. Being sincere. Smile. Being able to talk confidently to the prospect, or to the room full of prospects, or to the entire world in your website video. Showing yourself in all your glory is a terrific path to business success.

ZennaLude™

GO FOR THE GOLD! I have a real passion for increasing the number of people who have easy access to their authentic self a.k.a. their Best Self. I believe that the more people vibrantly living their truth, the better place this world can be. Not someone else's truth or story or mood. But their own. We aren't just here to buy houses or get legal counsel or receive business services or go to the doctor. That should be the icing - the gravy. The real gifts are the life experiences, learning, and connections we enjoy throughout our lives. We all know by now that life is about all the other stuff, right? You don't lie on your death bed and think "that house I sold in 1997 – wow that was great. And what a great real estate agent I had!" But if you gained a lifelong friend or warm relationship with that agent, well, you may be feeling grateful for THAT.

All the lessons we are here to learn, the friendships we are here to make, the life experiences and celebrations and triumphs that live in between all the 9-5 work related mumbo-jumbo – them's the gold. So when we encounter another human being interested in engaging with us on a human level WHILE they help get us through that compulsory societal mumbo-jumbo, well, it makes sense we'd rather do the mumbo-jumbo with them, right?

Chapter 4
The Business You Are Really In

By David Wolfe

You must understand you are in the marketing business. This truth collectively took me over fifteen years to understand. For many entrepreneurs, the message below may stir up indigestion. It goes *against* majority thinking. It goes against the way *most* businesses think.

Marketing for your business is not an isolated function like big corporations treat it. In their world, there is a department for advertising, a department for marketing, a department for sales, etc. Each is separate from the other, led by different people in different ways with, at best, connectivity but never integration. For you, marketing is the business with service deliverables secondary; marketing is seamlessly integrated with everything else. The appearance of the reception room, the scripts used by staff, and the chosen, practiced language of the consulting professional are as much marketing as the ad, website, brochure, shock and awe package, follow-up letters, etc. As Ray Kroc said, "Clean bathrooms is marketing, not sanitation."

EVERYTHING attracts or repels, sells or un-sells, strengthens or sabotages trust. Most professionals never break free of thinking like a deliverable a.k.a. providing consulting advice and services. Most label marketing as a nuisance and necessary evil versus thinking of themselves as a marketer of certain deliverables. This is a prison in many ways. It reinforces the dreaded work-money link. Our mission has been to guide people away from the common ways of regarding themselves, their professions, or their businesses to this other, uncommon mindset.

If you don't look at your business through the eye of a marketer, then you will always *just* be a technician and you will have to beg for customers. The sooner you accept that EVERY single piece of your business functions as marketing, the sooner you will be able to succeed.

So...your video presence is, or should be, a major component of your marketing strategy. It doesn't matter what business you are in. You must be able to articulate your message and do so naturally, and authentically, without being pushy or false. If you are 'old' like me, go back and read Chapter One. The world has changed so this means you also need to change even if you are already making bank and doing well. I made this change at the age of 49 close to ten years ago. I wish I would have had this book and my relationship with Kate at that time. Would have saved me a lot of time and anguish – and money.

Chapter 5
Making Money and Growing Your Business

By David Wolfe

You probably use email right now, yes? Probably two decades ago, there was a day when you decided to (finally!) get an email account. Prior to that, you met people in person or had phone conversations. But EVERYBODY was using email and you didn't want to miss the bus so you joined the 90s. Well, Buster – you are at that same crossroads right now. EVERYBODY is using video. The good news for you is that most people's videos are not that good. That might even be why you are not employing this communication medium: You don't want to come across like them. I get it...

I realize you may not be good at being in front of the camera right now. But if you look back over your life, there were plenty of things you were not good at but you got started learning anyway and, over time, became proficient at some and possibly a master at others. I remember when I started learning how to play guitar in the early 1990s. I was at a client site in Dallas and I was talking to one of the IT guys who said to me, "Learning to play guitar is difficult until it isn't". Same goes with being in the studio and appearing natural on camera.

Whether you realize it or not, you are competing against people or companies who *do* have a video presence. Even if their presence is not good, at least they have a video presence and, accordingly, a marketing leg up on you. For years my software consulting company, Lupine Partners, has had this competitive advantage because I was able to get past my fears and begin creating videos. Granted they were not terrific, but I still had a differentiator. Don't be left behind.

When I first started creating videos, I was VERY concerned about how I would come across to my competitors. I don't know why – it certainly isn't who I am now. I didn't want to be made fun of. Well that never happened or, if it did, I certainly don't remember it now. All I know is that my business was resuscitated. Prospects started opting in to my website where they could get free educational videos. Many were converted into paying customers. Stop and think about it: What the hell do you care about the other sheep crowding your market space? Trust me, they don't give a damn about you. While you may be friendly they probably aren't your friends. Why would you hide your greatest asset? That great asset being your unique personality and experience. Why?

I've always liked coloring outside the box. And videos have allowed me to do that – to be different, a maverick, to go where my competitors won't go. And now, with Kate's help, I am able to come across as I am naturally. Confident, self-assured, and dedicated to helping my customers and employees improve. It really is okay to upset industry norms. Who said that CPAs shouldn't have a video? Who said you can't create educational videos that attract prospects to you because you have entered the conversation that is going on inside their head?

Having videos also makes recruiting easier because future employees have a chance to get to know you prior to the interview. I have books and videos that people can read or watch prior to meeting me for the first time. It makes that whole process a little less daunting and nerve racking for the person on the other side. You can even make personalized videos to send to the recruit before or after the meeting to further seduce them into working with you (assuming you want to hire them!)

One of the biggest mistakes I see people making in business is not having a Plan B. Bad things happen to good people all the time and you are sticking your head in the sand if you don't think that you will suffer business setbacks. It's a certainty and part and parcel of being an entrepreneur – whether it be as a realtor, consultant, or business owner. You must expand your marketing expertise and offerings to reduce your business risk. An important lesson I learned early on was that 'one size does not fit all'. Meaning you have to use different bait to attract different customers. In the video world that means having different and many videos to speak to your varied and different clientele. People buy for different reasons. I could also say people *need* you for different reasons.

Many complain about having a small prospect pipeline. This is an instance where size actually does matter. The size of your pipeline is directly proportional to the size of your bank account. A lot of people brag about the size of their client roster – for me that's just an eye roll. Your client roster is focusing on the past. Unless you have your clients on paid continuity, then your client list is old news. Your pipeline, however, is the future. Your future. The great thing with videos is that you can begin a conversation with your prospects by feeding small doses of educational information that shows you as an expert. You are also building a reciprocity dynamic with your hoped-for future clients because they will begin to feel that they are in debt to you as a result of the free information you have given to them. I have been doing this for the past ten years and it is a winning strategy. The 'Taliban Videos' (see Chapter 8) were made with this in mind. I picked eighty educational topics and with my daughter Maggie we filmed those over one miserable day in late December many years ago.

I'll end with this: Do you remember the old *Peanuts* comic strip? The one where Lucy asks Charlie Brown to kick the football. He is wise to her antics as she always pulls the football away at the last moment and he falls on his ass. Not this time, she promises. He relents, goes up to kick the ball and, of course, she pulls it away. I had this comic strip on my wall for years as a reminder of why people don't like to buy – because they are afraid that the seller is going to 'pull the football away' and not provide what they promised. It's one of the reasons why Kate and I offer a complete, 100% refund after a studio session if our client does not feel that they received the value they expected. We would consider it stealing if we had an unhappy client. Are you resisting coming into the studio because you think somebody is going to pull the football away? Or is the resistance more geared towards looking silly or being out of your comfort zone?

ZennaLude™

TECHNOLOGY IS A GIFT NOT A CURSE! *It allows us to leverage our time like never before. We've had video, film, and TV for years but only recently have these communication modes been totally consumable by all through the wonders of widely available high-speed internet and cellular service. Everyone (except David's father and my father) has a smartphone. Everyone watches video daily either on TV, a computer, or smartphone or tablet. And even more people are watching video on platforms like Twitter, Facebook, Instagram, and Snapchat. Why not consider how valuable these outlets and opportunities are and recognize them as 'employees' who can help you share your message with thousands of people at a* time? Having a great video out there is like having a team of sales people ready to share with others how great you are at what you do. And it's a lot easier and cheaper than hiring all those sales people!

Chapter 6
Practical Business Applications for Your Videos

By David Wolfe

Here are some of the ways I have used videos in my consulting practice over the past ten years:

Company movie. Kate and I created videos for both businesses I am involved with – Lupine Partners and ZennaWolfe. The beauty of these videos is that it tells our stories and describes what we do. The movies are professional and they show us as the human beings who we are. It's a great brochure for our services. And they are easier to create than you think. The ZennaWolfe video was made in one studio day and the Lupine Partners movie was over 1.5 days. Very fun and cool.

Video business cards. These are just what they say there are. They replace the 'About Us' section on a website with you talking to your audience about who you are, what you do, and what your passions are. Most of our clients are hiring us to create these types videos. Kate even includes a link to her VBC in her email signature. The possibilities and applications are endless. If you create these video business cards, you will definitely have a leg up on your competition. It will also give your prospects a chance to 'know' you even before you have your first phone conversation or in-person meeting. Trust me, they will watch it before the meeting. Don't believe me? Reverse the situation. Imagine that you were going out to their website or LinkedIn to see who you were going to be talking to and they had a link to a video. Would you watch it? As they say on *Fargo*, "You betcha!"

Education. As you will find out later in this book, I began my video world by creating hundreds of educational videos for the purpose of building reciprocity with my prospect base. These videos also allow me to demonstrate authority as an expert in my field. I have over a hundred 30-75 second videos on implementing and migrating software systems. These videos also give my prospects the ability to meet me and like me. To get a sense of who I am. This educational route is a savvy marketing play and one that has made me a lot of money over the years. If you just made one video per week, at the end of one year you would have 52 of them. One video. Per week. That's worth an hour of your time in my opinion. What wallet-draining activity would you be willing to stop in order to create this single video each week?

Emails. Ever think about sending a video instead of an email? I've done it a few times for special situations. It is surprisingly easy to do – there are lots of companies that provide this service now. I have received <u>one</u> in my career and it shocked the hell out of me (in a good way). I was impressed that somebody would go through that much trouble. So, I decided to embrace the tactic myself and, in doing so, found out that it really wasn't that difficult.

Shock and awe package. The idea of a shock and awe package is pretty simple. It is to arrive in the prospect's hands with something that immediately sets you apart from everybody else trying to sell them anything. It preconditions the prospect to view you as an authority figure. They are 'shocked' and 'awed'. I always include specially-selected videos in my shock and awe packages. These take a little bit of time to create, but they have a HUGE ROI once you begin sending them out. Even the cover letter can be a video…I've done it!

Part II – David's Story

"One of the most beautiful compensations in life is that no person can help another without helping themselves."

Ralph Waldo Emerson

Chapter 7
Looking into the Mirror

By David Wolfe

During our first studio shoot, Kate and I were looking at some of my footage on the playback monitor during a break. I quickly noticed that there was an expression that I would make when thinking or trying to be cute or clever. And I made the face a lot – enough so that at some point Kate paused the playback and said, "What on earth is that face you keep making? Where did that come from? That's not YOU! And it certainly isn't serving you." This was the first of many times that Kate would mentor me when she thought I was being inauthentic on camera.

What she didn't know at the time was that someone close to me makes the same expression. The same tic. Apparently, I have been doing this for many decades and I picked it up from this person. I NEVER knew I was making the face. After going through this experience with Kate, I asked some of my employees if they have ever seen me make this face. They all answered 'yes'. Horrors.

Kate, because she is incredibly brilliant and is a monster dragon-slayer in the studio, said it was something I learned to keep myself down. To be self-deprecating. To not 'get above my raising' or to be too big for my britches. Which was definitely a lesson from my childhood. Being humble is not a horrible thing, but I did not want to be seen in public with that stupid expression on my face!

So, I decided to go to work on eliminating this from my life. First, I went back and watched all the videos to date. There was certainly more good than bad – but the bad was really bad. I was able to figure out the trigger that would occur in my head right before I made the face. I could manufacture that scenario in my mind and then for six straight Sunday mornings, I practiced not making the face. While I was doing this, I would read positive affirmations that Kate had written to me about how amazing I was and that the world needed for me to shine. And you know what? I broke this habit. I can't even make that facial expression anymore because I completely eradicated it from my being. Every now and then I feel that old 'friend' trying to peek through but he's pretty much been retired to the lower-most basement of my persona.

Here's what's important about all of this: I never would have known how I was hurting myself unless I had seen myself on camera. The camera acts as a mirror. It misses nothing and therefore catches everything. Which is a reason why people hate to see themselves on camera. So why not turn that around and use it as a tool for self-improvement in both your personal and professional life?

Once you have been coached and gone through the studio experience, your confidence is going to skyrocket. And this is true even if you have a lot of confidence. I have long said that I have more confidence than actual talent. But it's even higher since I became partners with Kate. I see it on camera, making in-person presentations, running meetings, and speaking in public. The reason is that I now know EXACTLY how I am coming across because I have seen myself on video so many times at this point. I like THAT David and it shows when I am in professional and personal situations.

Chapter 8
The Story behind the Taliban Videos:

Remembrances by Maggie Wolfe

From David: "Maggie and I knocked out 78 videos one December day between Christmas and New Year's Day. These videos are now known as the Taliban videos (because it looks like I have been taken hostage and I am recording a video to show that I am 'well'. Very easy to imagine a terrorist off to the side with an AK-47 pointed at me). These video days were always 'groan' days for me when I woke up. I normally lie in bed and mentally go through my 'to-do's' when I first get up. On my video days, I would say, "Darn, I have to do videos today...Ughh". When Kate first met me she said, "You look angry on camera". I WAS angry. Nothing ever worked. There were endless instances of teleprompter malfunction, Maggie giggling or saying "uh-oh". Shadows. Hissing sounds. Me forgetting lines. Any and everything that could go wrong would. I came to expect failure and it was usually written all over my face. The tension of knowing in advance that nothing would go smoothly.

It never crossed my mind to go to the studio."

I don't think the camera we were using was quite up to par and the beige background paper we chose was an abysmal failure. It was decidedly unstimulating and did nothing to make Dad look better. The camera stand was a table with boxes stacked up to get the camera to the correct height. We used Velcro and string to 'jimmy' the camera to get it placed just right. The entire setup was tenuous – we walked lightly and made sure we didn't sneeze. It was all very shaky. The lights were tethered to the wall with string.

Dad always wanted the 'set' to be ready at a certain time. He wanted to walk down, stand in front of the camera, do his recordings and then go back to his desk. That NEVER happened. Not one time. There was always some unforeseen problem. It made him crazy. Sometimes he looked so mad on camera – because HE WAS SO ANGRY! I was not responsible for Dad's mood. He would go from tense to moments of silliness and then back to tense. Then there was relief once we got to the last video. A mood of "let's just get this done so we can get back to our regularly scheduled programming"

Taliban picture on the left and a Kate Zenna-coached David on the right. (David is actually 7 years older in the picture on the right...)

A few times the ridiculousness of our setup would cause me to giggle right in the middle of Dad recording a video. I would try so hard to stifle this uncontrollable giggling – because of the craziness of it all – trying to make myself as silent and small as I possibly could. He would be furious with me! Once you start the giggles, you can't stop even when your Dad is giving you the death glare. Another time he had recorded a 'successful' take (successful in that he got through it with no fumbles even though he looked like the walking dead) and after he was done, I realized I had not hit the Record button. I said, "Uh-oh". His head shot up. "What?" "I forgot to hit the record button." A torrent of obscenities from the old man's mouth. I think that was the one that just about broke his back.

I remember one time after the recording was done and I was editing the videos, I kept hearing this sound on one of the videos. I took the videos to Dad and he listened. He was equally puzzled. Then he did the 'ah-hah' thing. The microphone was tucked inside of his jacket and it was picking up the sound of his stomach grumbling. He was hungry! Poor fella.

Then there was the cinder block tower. In one of our most comical attempts at production, Dad had me go out and buy a boatload of cinder blocks to 'fix' our stupid setup we had for getting the camera and teleprompter aligned. This 'tripod' was about five feet tall and three feet wide – a fortress! We moved it into one of the spare offices. We spared no expense in lighting and backdrops. Finally, we had a video and taping room! Except that room, as it turned out, was unbearably hot once the lights were turned on. Dad would have sweat POURING off him. I think we tried two shoots in there before he said 'screw it'. I think those were the last videos we did at the office. I think the cinder block fiasco was the final straw…I did everything I could to make those cinder blocks work. Darn it! (*Comment from David: It took me a year and a half to get rid of the cinder blocks through the trash one block at a time.*)

I think we did get some decent footage despite all of our missteps. When Dad would pump up the energy and focus, we got some pretty good videos. And I was able to get better at Premier Pro, which was a big help, too

So, do I miss working with Dad on these videos? Uh, that would be NO. I love him but I've done my time. He has teamed up with Kate and now he only works in the studio. I've earned my scar tissue with The Old Man.

Chapter 9
It's Never Too Late

By David Wolfe

People my age (I'm 58) talk about retiring. (Note: Do NOT include me in this group of people.) Or how they would like to play piano, or start a business, or get thinner, or (fill in the blank). But that it's too late for them, because they are too old. My response: Life is long. There is always time.

I recently read an article in *The Washington Post* about a 91-year-old man whose first novel had just been published. He's already working on his second novel. He sits down to write every day, seven days a week. He no longer gets up at 6:00 a.m. (slacker!); nowadays, he gets up at about 10:00 a.m., does a mile on the treadmill, and then starts writing. He gave up smoking ten years ago and still enjoys pastrami sandwiches and fries for lunch.

That's the guy I want to be. Somehow along the way, he figured out a life he wanted and has just kept on living it. He is happier getting things done than by being retired. He's a guy who's excited about what's next, not just about what's happened.

There are so many inspirational examples of people who accomplish great things later in life. Colonel Sanders started franchising KFC restaurants when he was 65. Michelangelo was also 65 when he finished the frescoes in the Pauline Chapel, and he continued designing masterpieces until his death at 88.

Grandma Moses took up painting when she was 80. George Burns continued to entertain up to his death at 100.

What's my next act? I'm not sure yet. I still play guitar. I still ride motorcycles for long distances and at very high speeds. I am learning to play the piano. I will always work at Lupine Partners. Here is what I am sure of: You can make whatever changes you really want to make in your life – it's never too late, it's not too hard, and it's not too crazy. Those are illusory barriers. You're not too old, you're not too busy, and you're not dead yet.

What about you? Are you too old for self-improvement? What's YOUR next act? Does going into the studio fill you with dread or give you the all-too-familiar pit in your stomach? I am walking testimony to the fact that you can start anything new at any point in your life.

It's never too late.

ZennaLude™

IT'S NEVER TOO LATE FOR ZENNA TO LEARN A THING OR TWO ABOUT A THING OR TWO. When DW suggested that we team up to create a business that connects his professional tribe with my professional tribe, I thought "Sure, sounds like fun, but how? I don't know the first thing about producing a shoot." Where do we do it? How do I find a studio? The crew? How much do you pay them? What kind of cameras and lights? Oh, we have to feed the crew? What's a gaffer? No way. Too much to handle for me, too much to learn. Well, lucky for all of our clients to date, my epic strain of stubbornness mixed with a need to succeed allowed ZennaWolfe to figure it out. We made misstep' but it was worth learning from experience. Now we pride ourselves on creating healthy, enthusiastic, positive studio environments for everyone – client and crew. Our studio culture is 'all hands on deck', no complaints, fun abounds and plenty of organic food for all to enjoy to keep our energy revved up. Because I jumped in and learned and was willing to fail, we gained so much. We gained a company. We only invite crew and professional film/TV artists who are willing and able to focus and share their talents with our clients. It's not an ego-thumping, self-congratulatory council ring of rock-star productions professionals. We come together to learn as much from our clients as we hope to offer in return. Now, if I had been lazy and outsourced all of this to an outside production company, we'd be missing out big time and so would our clients.

Part III
Taking the Next Step

"Do the thing you fear and the death of fear is certain."

Ralph Waldo Emerson

*Kate and David at the end of a long shoot
in August, 2015*

Chapter 10
But I'm No Good in Front of the Camera

By David Wolfe

But I'm no good in front of the camera, we hear…

What – you were born that way? Doled the not-good-in-front-of-the-camera gene? Nonsense. Here's the deal: We all have a baggage of crap we drag around with us – from childhood, from our well-meaning 'friends', co-workers, spouse, children, and parents. We're too fat, too ugly, have acne, receding hairline, crooked teeth. We forget things, we blush. And so on and so on. And then you add to all your baggage the fact that you are talking to a camera – a piece of plastic – with people sitting around you as you do it. Could ANYTHING be more unnatural?

The answer to that question could very possibly be *yes*. There is nothing more unnatural than sitting and talking to a camera. (Hint: Don't just stare into the camera lens like a psycho. When you are talking to a person face to face, do you stare at their eyes the entire time? No, you don't. You make eye contact then you look away and think and then you look back. While this is getting more advanced, think about how you would talk to somebody normally and then adopt that into your video practice. The difference in your final product will be much improved if you don't just stare into the camera. THAT is the most unnatural part.)

Here's the big secret – and I learned it from Kate. Nobody, except for a very few special folks, are naturally good in front of the camera. Our actor-coaches and Kate have worked at it – a lot and for a long time. You don't need years of acting training like they have, but you do need a couple of hours to get cozy with a camera alongside a skilled and compassionate professional coach. You also need a few mental hooks or tools that you can carry with you. Our coaches are absolute geniuses at locating your anxiety points and working with you to lower, if not eliminate, your anxiety. I have experienced the anxiety personally and watched many, many people in the studio transform themselves.

Each and every one of them told us that they were "no good in front of the camera."

So there.

ZennaLude™

PERMISSION TO SPEAK FREELY? Permission granted. Yes. I have officially granted you <u>permission to be yourself on camera</u>. Yup. I said that. Let me say it again. I grant you permission to be yourself on camera. Everything YOU are is EXACTLY what we and the camera (and your clients) want to see. Imagine that the lens is your mother and father the day after you were born. Full of love for you. Brimming with pride. Nothing you did was wrong. You provided only joy. All your wrinkles, and bald baby head, and challenging smells...perfection! When we are ourselves and in the moment, that's when we rock the lens.

Sometimes I work with people who have a challenge letting themselves be beautiful, to shine, to feel good about what they are doing and talking about, to speak with confidence in their tone of voice. Not everyone feels highly passionate about their work, job, or offered services all the time. Once I remind them why they are pursuing their career, all the people who benefit from their efforts, I can get them to remember why they came to us in the first place. It can't ever just be about the money. It's got to be about YOUR clients. Then, I remind them, they have been granted permission...go beckon your clients freely!

Chapter 11
Fear, a Tool Belt, and Jose Cuervo

By Kate Zenna

What do you do when you have a client who has TREMENDOUS fear in front of the camera? Not everybody is like David Wolfe who madly charges toward his fear. Most of us avoid what we fear at all costs, myself included – I am a master at avoiding learning any kind of time-management system! I fear I will lose the benefits of living spontaneously and creatively. I'm sure I'd end up creating more free time to be spontaneous; but I can be stubborn. That came with the Kate Zenna package. When working with David on-camera, all I have to do is tease him so he laughs and doesn't come across as a grumbling sourpuss like he did before he met the likes of me. Perhaps, one day, I'll be tricked into easily enjoying the learning of new time management systems!

Last year, while coaching software consultant superstar Amy Beesley, I had to navigate her extreme fear around a camera. Amy is both wildly intelligent and very 'cool'. She was talkative and expressive off-camera but once she heard "action!" she froze up and her entire body language screamed 'brace for impact'. I used many tools before I came to the one that 'spoke' to Amy. It's the last one I mention in this little essay.

Often, the first tool I use is logic. I remind my clients that it's just a camera – a cheap piece of plastic probably made in China. It can't hurt you let alone kill you. And if you botch a take or a moment, nobody has to see it. There's no law that says every take has to rock the lens. There is no need for you to be embarrassed. That's what the editing room is for. We will cut around any bits that aren't super flattering to you. Just like what happens in Hollywood...

If logic isn't working, then I often use emotion to pry out the most engaging spirit of a client. Some clients tend to default to a negative or less-positive emotional state. DW is one of these people. There's nothing wrong with that, it simply means I have to lure him into a very happy place immediately prior to filming, even if he's communicating a serious message to the camera. I learned early on with David that my best strategy with him was to make him laugh – fortunately something I can do quickly and easily. Once I get him laughing, I say "action" and he begins his on-camera message with the signature DW twinkle in his eyes. That twinkle-in-the-eye-enthusiasm is the authentic David, but he needs me and the other coaches at ZennaWolfe to consistently bring it out. And, to his credit, I now see him getting better at starting from that perspective when a camera is around (or even in a meeting).

A lot of camera fear is birthed during childhood. Years ago, before I knew I would become so comfortable in front of a camera, I had a major bone to pick with any camera or any person toting a camera. From the ages of about 10 to 17, much to my parent's dismay, I would remain in my bedroom as guests would arrive at our house and, as a result there are very few photos of me during that time. I couldn't bear to withstand the pressure I'd feel when I was introduced by my mother to a room full of her friends or even extended family. Since then, I've done a lot of thinking about this and I now feel pretty comfortable with the likely reasons for this behavior. What remains curious to me is why, at the age of 19, while attending

Queens University in Canada, did I suddenly become completely committed to becoming a film and TV actor? It was more than a dedication or commitment; it was knowledge that *this* was who I was and who I would become. I'm not sure I'll ever really know the answer to this. It was as much a shock to me as it was to my parents who were beaming at their future lawyer daughter! The challenge soon became to find a way to reverse my lifelong discomfort with being in front of people. I had plenty of excuses to feel justified in my discomfort – I was six feet tall (including my slouch!), I had one eyebrow thanks to my Greek heritage and I, apart from swimming, had almost zero athletic abilities, which meant I had zero comfort in my physical body. Luckily for me, I was born with an extra helping of stubbornness that allowed me to try and fail but never give up on my dedication to the craft of acting.

My job as a coach involves being a bit of a psychologist for my clients as well. What is their issue? What are their self-image problems (because we ALL have some!)? Two of my favorite tried-and-true techniques when digging for the gold of someone's personality are:

One – Question and Answer format. I will engage the client in a discussion with me and have the cameras rolling. At some point, they will forget the camera is there and with proper editing the person's essence and realness will shine through. Most people forget about the camera after five minutes, which is when all the fun begins.

Two – Host the Party (see Chapter 21). When you're hosting a party, you open the door and say, "Hi! How are you? Come in, come in". Or, if you're already in the party and someone introduces you to one of your guests and you say 'hello' and start chatting with them, you're probably very welcoming. You offer a warm vibe. You've put food out. Maybe you've got margaritas made. You're using your grandmother's punch bowl (or maybe that's just me). You've taken a lot of time to welcome your guests and treat them specially. Well, the same thing goes for when you're on-camera.

Now back to Amy Beesley! I admit that for a while during our session, I struggled in getting her to be the same person on-camera as she was off-camera. So what finally worked? I was teaching her how to host the party and I inspirationally asked, "Do you drink?" "Yes," she replied. "What did you drink?" "Shots," she said with confidence. "What kind of shots?" "Usually Jose Cuervo," She beamed. And beamed…

"Action!" Night and day difference. Amy nailed it. Being a ZennaWolfe coach requires having many tools in our tool belt. Even tequila, and arguably, especially tequila!

Chapter 12
Is it Real or is it Imagined?

By David Wolfe

At some point in my life (although I will say it was within the past five years and I'm 58 years old as I write this), I learned this technique for assuaging anxiety – when I feel the pressures building up. I sit and purge every single thing that is bothering me. I don't filter and am not logical. I just write out whatever is bothering me. I purge it out through my fingers on to a piece of paper. A lot of people do this but they stop with this first step.

Step two is taking your list of grievances and issues and breaking them down into two groups: real and imagined. Did something *really* happen that is causing your stress and distress or did you just work up a doozy in your mind? I have put fifteen to twenty people through this exercise and every single time the ratio is 80/20 imagined events to real life. This was also the ratio each and every time I do this for myself.

Stop reading and do this now. You can either do it around a specific area in your life or you can just focus on this notion of being in front of the camera, making a speech, or anything where you have a bunch of people looking at you.

You will probably feel some discomfort. That's okay – in fact, it's good. Now ask yourself: Are these anxious or fearful feelings real? Are you actually in danger? (Real) Or are you imagining failure and ridicule from your somewhat-well-meaning family, friends, and peers? What would happen if somebody did bust your balls about your camera presence? Would you die?

Time and time again Kate and I have watched VERY nervous clients walk into our studio and a few hours later walk out on top of the world with a boatload of new skills, because they realized that the fear they had in their mind was not real. They made it up. Once slayed it is slayed forever.

These imaginary fears are the primary reason why we are so comfortable giving a 100% guarantee on our coaching and studio fees. The transformation is so compelling and our clients are so sky-high after the sessions, the thought of asking for a refund is unfathomable. We have the before and after videos from our clients as proof.

Chapter 13
On Growth

By David Wolfe

For years I have made this statement to my consulting staff: With growth comes tension. It's true. There is tension around getting out of your comfort zone. In walking through that mirror of fear. Emerson said, "Do the thing you fear and the death of fear is certain." We've all experienced this. We DREAD doing something and spend all sort of emotional and psychological currency thinking about this thing we don't want to do. Then we do it and it's never even close to as bad as we thought it was going to be.

Same thing when contemplating going into the studio to get some training.

In our company movie at www.zennawolfe.com, Kate, at the very end of the film, uses the phrase "…unfold like a flower…" when describing the beauty of watching our clients evolve with a little help from us. Going in front of the camera takes some bravery. You WILL grow. I put my first day in the studio with Kate very high on my list of growth opportunities. Creating my first video on my own took bravery. Even though I failed. Even though I felt tension. You feel tension and then you grow.

Making the decision to improve yourself through personal examination and facing the mirror of fear (which the camera makes you do) will give you the opportunity to see how you present yourself to the world and will also give you the gift of self-improvement. It's a form of therapy. One that you don't have to go to for years to be 'cured'. One session, maybe two in the studio with a professional actor-coach should be enough to see amazing improvement and personal growth.

ZennaLude™

A PERFECTIONIST'S COUNTERINTUITIVE ADDICTION TO PERSONAL GROWTH. Many of us are afflicted with the need to be perfect. This need is often cultivated during childhood and sometimes it creates exceptionally driven and professionally successful people. It can also be our Achilles heel when it comes to personal growth. Most commonly, in order to surpass various accomplishments and continue the mountain climb to additional successes and triumphs, we must undergo fairly rigorous personal growth. You can imagine how perfectionism and personal growth can cause some friction in our lives since the first part of growth is to learn that you are not perfect!

As a self-admitted (and friend-confirmed) perfectionist and personal-growth champion, I have had many challenges balancing my need to get outside my comfort zone and my need to be great. To help me with this challenge, I do what I can to surround myself with inspiring, strong, talented, and courageous people. I adore my actor colleagues for their steady display of bravery, whether it's at auditions or simply sticking with their chosen career path despite its guarantee of multiple heartbreaks. I also surround myself with people outside of the arts who demonstrate a strong willingness to grow personally and professionally.

I have a friend, who, if you met him or saw him out during a business lunch, you would NEVER, EVER, EVER think that he is someone who annually attends the Burning Man festival in the California desert or that he consults privately with a Kundalini Yogi and Tony Robbins, practices Martial Arts, is a dedicated father and community supporter, or smokes the occasional cigarette! This friend is an example of someone who provides me with tremendous inspiration to continue to grow on a personal level (which always leads to professional growth, by the way). I hope you can imagine the kind of growth it's taken to finally get me to sit down and write this book! Well, that and also being partners with David Wolfe who is a tremendous support and source of encouragement and inspiration.

Knowing myself and being able to see what personality traits may hold me back from the next accomplishment has been something that has arrived through tremendous personal-growth efforts. I love my perfectionist strengths for all the obvious reasons but I must admit, I love my never-ending desire for continued personal growth even more. If you are reading this, I know you are a comrade in this regard, otherwise you'd never have gotten this far in the book!

Chapter 14
Giving Yourself the Go-Ahead

By David Wolfe

I became a CPA in 1982 but, at the core, I have always been a software consultant – it's what I was meant to do. I started my own boutique software consulting firm, Lupine Partners, in 1993. I have been running the Software Professional Mastermind Group for over a decade. I have written three books – make that four with this little gem. I have earned a Quilly award as a Best-Selling author. I have been on Amazon's best-seller list as a contributor for the book *Out Front: Business Building Strategies from Frontline Entrepreneurs*. I have won two Telly awards as an Executive Producer on two Emmy-winning documentaries. I have walked on the Red Carpet. I have worked for famous people (John Connally and Steven Brill). Hobnobbed. On top of that, I am a husband, father, grandfather, guitar player, motorcycle rider, and a former marathon runner.

I have been told more than once that I would NEVER be able to do the type of marketing that I do. There was a time when I, too, would have been hesitant to market as aggressively as I do. There are a couple of reasons for that. One, it just seemed a bit unseemly – not very CPA-ish. Two, I was foolishly concerned with how I would be perceived by my professional peers. (Needless to say, this concern has been eradicated from my DNA.)

The single biggest change in my mindset over the last decade was the decision that I wasn't going to wait around anymore for anyone to give me permission to do anything. I wasn't going to wait for some publisher to ask me to write a book. I wasn't going to wait for some committee or group to anoint me 'important'. I wasn't going to wait and hope for clients to hire me. Instead, I was going to give myself permission to take action to change. I gave myself the Go-Ahead.

Give yourself the Go-Ahead. The go-ahead to get into the studio. The go-ahead to have a public face. The go-ahead to have a virtual face on the internet. The go-ahead to make more money. To walk through your own personal mirror of fear. To self-actualize and to live the fullest life possible.

ZennaLude™

GRATITUDE FOR A GO-AHEAD COACH NAMED DAVID WOLFE. *Just because I'm good at coaching on-camera professionals (actors) and novices (you!), doesn't mean I didn't have to learn the GO-AHEAD lessons taught to me by the Mighty Wolfe. Sure, over the course of my twenty-year acting career I've become adept at auditioning and not getting the job over and over and over...and OVER again. That's easy peasy stuff now. But I am just like you in that I had to go through a lot of 'inner turmoil' to get on board with the notion that I could own and operate a successful coaching and media production business. Every time I begin a day of coaching and directing, I take a few moments to quell my nerves that are screaming a steady stream of silly and untrue thoughts and uncertainty. But if I had cowered and given in to that fear, I never would have co-built ZennaWolfe. This would have meant that many people, including our crew members and our clients, would not have benefitted from all that ZennaWolfe offers. So thanks, Mighty Wolfe. Thanks for helping me leap off my plateau and learning how to ascend even higher.*

Chapter 15
Anxiety, a Friend

By David Wolfe

We all live in different places, are different ages, and have different businesses but every one of us has this in common – fear and/or anxiety. We have felt, do feel, and will feel it again. I feared the CPA exam, my first day working professionally, going out on my own, and – now that I have achieved all that I have – I have a whole new set of anxieties. Fear either mobilizes people or stops them dead in their tracks.

Entrepreneurs who end up being successful don't let fear paralyze them. The difference between us and other people is that we have learned and continue to learn how to channel our fear to motivate us.

It is how people like us get things done and come up with new ideas. All of those small businesses that have come up against a Walmart-like company entering their territory are prime examples of what I am talking about. Some of them threw up their hands and folded; others found way to refocus their businesses. For me, it was how, as a solo practitioner (which I was for five years), I could compete with the bigger consulting firms. I figured it out because I had to figure it out. I had two small children who were counting on me.

Whenever we hear FDR's famous quote about fear, we rarely hear the whole sentence: "The only thing we have to fear is fear itself, nameless, unreasoning, unjustified terror which paralyzes needed efforts to convert retreat into advance." Every time you feel that twinge of fear, use it as the great motivator it can be. Don't run from it; embrace it. Feel it. It is a gift that will give you an edge.

Real Life: Before hiring my first employee in 1998 I had EXTREME anxiety. I had scrimped and saved $35,000 over the previous five years and if this hire did not work out, then I would have probably lost all the savings. For me, this $35,000 was an enormous amount of money – particularly having gone bankrupt as a young man in my late 20s. Several years before this, I was reading Dear Abby one day in the paper and there was this line in one of her responses: "Regret is the cancer of life." I clipped that little sentence out and taped it to the refrigerator door. I saw that on the door one night and I decided that I would rather regret losing the $35,000 than regret not taking the chance. I made the hire, it was the right one, and I have never looked back.

Is anxiety a friend or a foe to you?

◊ ◊ ◊ ◊ ◊ ◊ ◊ ◊ ◊

ZennaLude™

SOMETIMES YOU JUST GOTTA GO FOR IT! I think one of the most memorable instances of where I found a way to use my anxiety and nerves to my advantage was when I was auditioning for a role on a CBS Movie of the Week. The role was a large one, for the best friend of the star who, at the time, I only knew would be a Hollywood actress. I was living in Toronto at the time and this was my first network TV audition, so I was in my right mind to be super-nervous! The character, Deanna, was a singer in a bar but I didn't have to sing to in the scene that I was auditioning. In fact, I wasn't even required to be able to sing, so you can imagine my surprise (and my perfectionist's meltdown!) when I heard the girl auditioning ahead of me singing AMAZING GRACE! I panicked and asked the other actors waiting if they knew about this and had prepared a song to sing. None had. Well, that made me feel better, but then, why was <u>that</u> girl singing in there?! Surely that meant that they really liked her? Now she's got a real leg up on me. That's terrible! How can I follow that act?

Although I sang in my own band, playing our own original songs, I was by no means a conventional singer. I didn't know one standard or cover song and certainly had nothing prepared. Well, I went in, did my audition and the Los Angeles producer who was there in the room thanked me – but <u>didn't ask me to sing!</u> Instead of racing out of that room, tail between my legs, feeling as though I failed for not getting his interest enough to ask me to sing, I stood there and asked him, 'Well, don't you want me to sing for you too?" As these words spilled from my mouth, my perfectionist side had a conniption. What was I thinking?! You don't HAVE a song to sing! Shut up, Zenna! The last time you attempted to sing Amazing Grace in front of a singing coach, she basically suggested that you <u>give up</u> singing and try tennis or anything else! Don't do it! Leave! NOW! Fueled by the power of nervous energy and my drive to succeed, I proceeded to sing (to my best recollection) 'Perfect' by an obscure 1980s band called Fairground Attraction. I even added a 'ba-boom-boom-boom-boom' to account for the drums between the verse and the chorus. It was ridiculous. But I totally went for it. I went kamikaze on that audition!

I left the room feeling a mix of euphoria and utter horror knowing that my agent would for sure be dropping me later that day when he heard of my behavior.

He did call a couple of days later to let me know that I had won the role! Seriously, I nearly did a backflip. (That role had me work opposite the lovely and talented Annabeth Gish and Jon Stamos, one of my teen heartthrobs – I'm so glad I went for it!)

This experience demonstrated to me a few things:
    1. Nervous energy IS your friend. It's your fuel, your fire, your ally.

2. *The only thing you have to stand out is YOU. You may as well show yourself just in case it's exactly what someone wants. (Usually they don't know what they want anyway, they're just looking for something amazing.) And if it's not, well, at least YOU had a fun time!*

3. *No matter how prepared you may be, things almost always shake out unexpectedly and you need to have #1 and #2 fully embraced so you can still have a great experience...and show others how to do it too!*

Chapter 16
On Being Timid

By David Wolfe

Occasionally, at software conferences, I am approached by other consultants. They come up to me and ask, "Do you have anything for me?" They are asking me if I have any consulting work I can slide their way. Any crumbs. They will 'consult for food'.

Every single time this happens, I ask them to keep me up to speed on a periodic basis as to their availability so I can keep them in mind. I promise you, not one time have any of these people followed up with me, written me a thank you note for my time, or offered any sort of quid pro quo. Sending me an email once a month to let me know they were finishing up a project and were available for work, asking if we had excess demand was just too much work for them. I used to tell them (I have since learned not to waste my time) to join one of my marketing groups. The response was ALWAYS – How much does it cost? Instead of: Could I learn to generate my own clients from your group? How much more in revenue could I expect to generate from what I would learn from you? I mean, who cares what it costs?

You and I are surrounded by people who are too timid, who accept the media's creative portraits as reality, and who let life push them around. These timid people leave their courage at home in a drawer, and as Zig Ziglar has said from many a stage, "Timid salesmen have skinny kids..."

This lesson is one I took to heart early on when I first started making changes in my professional and personal life and doing my own style of marketing. I have been held up to ridicule by my peers – those people who nod their heads and click their tongues at people who try new ideas. People either like me or REALLY don't like me. I don't care.

Know that your competitors are sitting around waiting for someone to show them what ought to be done and then to do it for them. They're the ones who are afraid of new ideas, who let the marketing sales reps write their ads, or who refuse to put some energy and effort into making the Internet a part of a sophisticated marketing plan or create a shock and awe package.

Also know that your competitors may be too timid to ever set foot into a studio. Or maybe they are arrogant. Or afraid of looking foolish. Would you rather be rich or right? Bold or timid?

Chapter 17
Everyone Needs a Coach

By Kate Zenna

As a veteran film and TV actor, I know that this reaction to a camera is completely unnecessary if you have learned some foundational tools that make the whole process fun. With the thousands of hours I've spent on-camera and around cameras, I've learned how to enjoy the experiences and to succeed as well. When I work with a client, there are four basic steps we work through during the day together.

Step 1. I get to know you. I hear from you what your concerns are. We may look at old footage you've shot. We talk about what you like about yourself on-camera or in front of people. We talk about what you'd like to improve. I begin to 'learn' my client during this process so I can find a way to access that most brilliant and shining side of them. Because that's what looks best on camera and it's what appeals to any audience.

Kate on set working her magic

Step 2. During this part of our process together we can be working on some copy that you are wanting to film. It may be an old video message or something you need to film soon. We will either begin to work on-set, or we'll begin to rehearse and run through the process. Once we get to set to start shooting, we'll feel very comfortable together and we can start to identify the strange things that start to affect most clients once the camera has shown up. Some clients are very knowledgeable about where their weak spots are – others have no idea. This is when I get to see what happens to them when cameras are rolling, the pressure is on, and all eyes are upon them.

All of my coaching tips are aimed at helping you let down your guard enough to let you be your best on camera and in front of people (to give you *permission* to be your best!). When you think about people who are 'at their best' while in front of others, what are the most common characteristics that come to mind? I've asked many people this question and the answers always include things like:

- they smile easily but genuinely
- they seem happy and fun
- they seem calm and confident
- they don't beat themselves up, they seem to like themselves
- they have good energy
- they seem very comfortable in front of the camera or in front of groups
- they take their time and speak audibly, not rushing or mumbling

These symptoms, or characteristics, of a person at their best are what we are all wanting to exhibit when we want to perform at our highest level. The fun part is decoding each of my clients to determine which tool will work best for each person. Often, as an actor working on set, it will take a few attempts by a director for them to get the desired performance out of me or any actor. That's because, as complex human beings, we are often not able to emotionally respond to intellectual things like *words*. That's why you often hear actors say things like, "Well, what's my motivation?" Motivation boils down to a *feeling*, an emotion and that is so much clearer to physically embody. When I work with clients who are seeking tools to specifically help them be more compelling on-camera, I often try a few different tricks. Eventually there will be one that will resonate. Often there are a few that the client responds positively to, which they recall later when they have to perform on their own.

Business videos are created as a way to expand business, correct? We do them to create another connection between ourselves and our prospects. They are a terrific tool because if you're able to connect with your tribe by video, to make them feel more comfortable with you, you have the potential to reach so many more people more profoundly than you would by phone or in person. In fact, I could argue that by video you have more to gain or lose because the prospect can re-watch you over and over again if they want to decide whether they can trust you. In person, they only have the one 'touch' to go by. So, if you're going to do video, be good at it! Take the time to take your time. One great way to make sure you take your time is to learn how to enjoy the whole process.

Step 3. This phase begins naturally at some point after I get on-set with a client. Once I see what happens when the lights are on, I can begin to work with various tools and techniques to get a client to be themselves. We work on the material the client has brought with them to shoot and we watch back on the monitor how slight changes in thought, perspective, posture or body position alters the result on video.

Role reversal. David directing Kate during the filming of the ZennaWolfe company movie

This part of our work can take a long time depending on how deeply my clients want me to help hone them. One of THE most important things to remember is I BEG MY CLIENTS TO NOT BE PERFECT. I IMPLORE THEM.

Step 4. I want to make sure clients have tools they can use on their own that will unlock their best self on camera when I'm not around to help. Unless I can train people to be self-sufficient in front of a camera, I don't feel we've been of service. The people I've coached express how their one session with me has forever bettered their ability to be themselves on camera. Just recently, a software consultant who was almost hopeless when I began working with her, had an on-camera experience that never could have happened without the rigorous training we did. This is what makes what I do so rewarding.

In the last part of my day with a new client, I discuss how they will handle working with a camera, a production crew, and/or a videographer going forward. We talk about how to prepare to work with people who will NOT have their back on set or on screen. I've learned this the VERY hard way…I need to know my best side, my best body position, my best neckline, and color or fabric for wardrobe. Even a hair stylist may not get my look right. Same with a makeup artist. This happens ALL the time.

For clients who are shooting their own videos, we frequently discuss how to make it a seamless process. For example, setting up a studio that's always ready to go with lighting is a great practice. We discuss how important good sound is and how to make that happen easily.

Chapter 18
Why Working Actors Make the Best Performance Coaches

By Kate Zenna

As an actor, my main job is to be believable as a character. How that's accomplished is equal parts skill, talent, and divine inspiration. One thing is certain, when we are working with other actors, we need to find a way to intimately connect with them very, very quickly. Whether we are a guest-star, co-star, or the star, we will have to play opposite other actors who are unfamiliar to us, who often we've met only minutes before our scene together. We will be required to make it seem as though we've worked together before, or we're longtime friends, or we're their parent or child!

This means we need to be able to instantly let our guard down enough to 'let them into our hearts'. I need to specifically connect with the person who is acting opposite me to make the scene and interaction feel believable to an audience. Yes, it means we need to listen, watch, and be 'in the moment' with the other actor; but it <u>also</u> means that we must be open and allow them to 'see into us' in return so that they can connect. Otherwise, the scene is about two people trying to connect rather than two characters (*played by two people)* interacting.

So, how does this translate into how our coaches work with clients on a ZennaWolfe set?

As actors, we are trained and innately geared toward connection, and we can feel it instantly when someone isn't being genuinely themselves. We are very sensitive to this. At one point in our training, we were there too, so we inherently know what it looks and feels like. We are so geared towards gaining a connection with the person opposite us that we are willing to do what it takes to make that happen. Usually we can do this without a client even being aware of what we are doing, which is fine. We have a limited amount of time to get a person to open up and reveal their best and most shiny selves on a set. So we have to be extremely seasoned in our ability and natural drive to 'connect' with the person.

One of my favorite acting coaches, Sandy Marshall, would constantly remind us in class, "Your job is to make the other actor fall for you. Your job is to be adorable!"

Kate directing a ZennaWolfe client
documentary film

When an actor is an auditioning machine (going out to an audition at least a few times a month), like most working actors are, they have strong 'connection muscles' as I call it. I truly believe that people who have been successful as film/TV actors are the best support a novice on-camera performer can hope to find. We've been there, done that and most likely STILL deal with our nerves and performance anxieties. In the case of ZennaWolfe clients, there's zero performance – it's all YOU. It's who you are that's going to rock the camera and that's who we will connect with – that's our promise!

Part IV
Lessons from a Professional Actor

"Every artist was first an amateur."

Ralph Waldo Emerson

Chapter 19
Becoming an Actor – the Early Days

By Kate Zenna

One of my missions is to help the people on this planet shine. I know that the world and everyone in it will benefit if we can raise the number of people who shine brightly. I've decided that a great way for me to succeed is to get as many people into our studios as possible. A camera can act like a drill sergeant in a way – demanding focus and attention while also enticing success with its inherent vibe of intimidation.

I was majoring in Human Geography (don't worry, you're not alone – I'm not sure what it is either) when I got hit by the acting bug. For me the bug hit me in the form of a very clear vision of me wearing a silvery, sequined dress singing on a stage. The vision gave me feelings of deep certainty that my future would be as an actor. Kevin Costner's *Dances with Wolves* had recently been released and, being a massive fan of his, I went to see that film in the theater, alone, close to a dozen times. Kevin's story of where he came from, how he pursued his career, and how he fought to write, produce, direct, *and* star in this epic film became my mantra in a way and he my silent mentor.

From that time on, I was singularly focused on becoming a professional film and TV actor. Had I known it would have been a full decade before I would get my first professional role, I doubt I would have continued. (If I'd known how much Invisalign™ would hurt and inconvenience me – same thing!) Oh, the gifts of naivety! When you're in love, nothing's going to stop you, right? And, so often, the pain required to succeed is worth it.

I auditioned for a local community theater production and won the role. It was my first real audition and I scored the gig. As far as I was concerned this acting thing was easy-peasy! I announced to my parents that I was going to leave university early to pursue acting. Luckily my mother had enough power over me to convince me to get my bachelor's degree before I ran off to be an actress. My grades went up from a C to a solid A-minus GPA because of my excitement, focus, and certainty. I finished my degree a few months later, spent the summer saving money while working at The Kingston Brewing Company, and headed across the country to Vancouver, British Columbia – one of Canada's largest film production hubs in the 1990s.

It was during this chapter of time when I auditioned for an acting and modeling agent who informed me, after my audition, that my reading was the worst audition he'd ever witnessed. Terrible, right? More on that story in the next chapter.

Along with learning to act, I had taught myself how to sing and had formed a band with a brilliant guitarist/musician. Despite more than one singing teacher gently suggesting that I quit singing, I co-founded a band. We called ourselves Far Gone and, to my delight, we managed to get some gigs in and around Vancouver. The first time I performed as a singer on stage singing my own original songs will remain one of the coolest moments of my life. I didn't have traditional vocal talent and I didn't know a single cover song. My musical idols were Sinead O'Connor, Morrissey and Matt Johnson from the English band, The The. My idols were all from the UK music of the 1980s. One day, I heard The Cranberries on the radio, phoned (on a landline!) my band partner and said, "Quick!! Turn on the radio! That's the kind of music I want to make." So, while I was learning the ropes of acting (meaning auditioning and not getting jobs), I was at least making music.

After enduring six years in the rainforest that is Vancouver, it occurred to me that I may prefer to see the sun a little more often and that it may be wise for me to try another acting city. I still didn't have an agent and was on the brink of quitting, but I wanted to give it one last shot. So, I packed up and hauled back east to Toronto. Toronto turned out to be a smart move and, within a year, I found my way to a non-union audition for a little Canadian feature film called *Jack and Jill* that would lead to my nomination for a Canadian Academy Award for Best Supporting Actress. My first agent soon followed along with great auditions and more than a few roles that finally went my way.

I hope that you may derive something from my story that sparks you to pursue your current charm, something that nudges your great idea or deep passion into full gear. Our world needs YOU to be turned on, to *shine*, to create solutions and inspiration. I need you. Because *your* shine will inspire *my* shine. It is my passion to help YOU and your dreams and your genius to come alive in this lifetime. All I do, every business, every venture, each initiative has this purpose at it its core. *This* is how we connect. And through connection, and only through connection, may we enjoy the greatest bounty that being alive offers and that is to experience the fullest spectrum of love.

Chapter 20
Get Back On That Horse

By Kate Zenna

Not long ago, I had a client who came to us because she had to record a video presentation for her business. She had had a horrible experience years before that led her to freezing up, being nervous, and not being herself. So she came to us. The video she now wanted to create was an internal presentation for her company that would end up on the company website with all employees watching it for years and years to come. She wanted to make sure she did her best for this for all the obvious reasons. Because 'what happens in the studio stays in the studio,' I won't go into exact detail around her challenges, but I want to share with you a story that this client found very helpful in her session.

This client had tremendous nervous energy and a significant nervous tic that came out when she was on-camera. It was something that only happened when her nerves were on high alert and seeing the evidence on-screen was understandably mortifying for her. Luckily, she was aware of the situation, which is what prompted her to come to us to help relieve it.

I told her my humiliating story of my first agent audition. When I began auditioning for acting jobs in Vancouver, I went to some auditions from ads I found in the newspaper. I managed to get myself in front of a decent-sized acting and modeling agent despite my lack of experience and only minimal training. I had been in two plays while at university – that was the extent of my training and experience. I definitely had more gumption than actual experience. The agent who agreed to meet me gave me some lines to read and I was told to memorize them if I could and, in ten minutes, I would perform the scene. I sat across from the agent and played my role. As it was happening, I remember thinking I was in the zone. I could feel how *naturally* I was saying the words. The agent, however, looked down and seemed very uncomfortable. He said to me, "That was by far the worst scene reading I have ever experienced." I thought he was joking! Surely I couldn't possibly be the WORST! That seemed a bit exaggerated. In shock, I calmly uttered, "Okay, I'll go and get some training and see you in six months." I fled that penthouse office and, before the elevator hit the ground, my face was drenched in a torrent of tears beneath my sunglasses. Luckily, I somehow decided that that experience, as horrible it was, was going to lead me to a successful career as an actor. I thought, "Now I have really great first-audition story to tell!"

My lesson from this is to just get back on the horse. Shame on that person who spoke to me the way he did. He was unnecessarily cruel. Not a good guy. When you have a bad performance experience, get back in the ring or, in this case, the studio. Don't let one bad performance taint your desire to improve and grow.

When it comes to performing for the camera, there is always room for great improvement. No matter how many flubs or less-than-perfect takes, you only get better with practice. The funny thing is, when clients come to me and beat themselves up for not being great on-camera right away, I remind them that I've had over twenty *years* of training and experience and I still make mistakes – all the time! I mess up lines, lose focus, allow my self-consciousness take over my brain, have self-doubt…All. The. Time! Once I fully convince our clients that they too can learn to enjoy these pitfalls – and that only when they surrender to the flubs as they inevitably happen – will the great shine arrive.

And one more thing…

It's VIDEO! We can cut. We can edit. We can snip around an 'um', or 'you know', or 'like' or a random look up to the sky when you're thinking. Say yes to the wipe outs and enjoy the ride, because that's the trick to the whole thing! You don't have to be perfect but, through the process, you're definitely going to learn how to make your communications better.

Chapter 21
Host The Party!

By Kate Zenna

No matter what you're doing, no matter what you're shooting on-camera, I want to help you realize that the people you are speaking to are coming to your 'party'. So host it. It's that simple.

Hosting the party started with me as an actor because I would constantly go into audition rooms and the people who are making the decision about whether or not I get a job are often a group of people who are busy, tired, and have seen a lot of actors throughout the day. The vibe when I go into those rooms can be really, really unwelcoming. If I let the mood of the room get to me, I will be thrown off. So, instead, I take control of the energy in the room.

For a long time, I would get insecure and thrown off by the bad vibe that was in the room until I realized, "Wait a second, I'm in control of this space." I'm in control of my life. If I walk in and I decide to host the party instead of being a guest at <u>their</u> party, the whole thing changes. So, I give them a vibe of welcoming love and it calms them down – it makes them think, "Oh, what's going on?" Suddenly, I become more interesting to them. I'm more comfortable and having a better time because I'm hosting a party, and I can go quietly about my business knowing that this is my space right here. I am allowing *you* to come into it. I am welcoming <u>you</u>.

So, extending this to you, if you're doing a presentation for work and there are all these people slumped over, on their phones, typing on the computer, and no one really cares, don't take that personally. Shame on them for not having more enthusiasm in their day, but why don't you teach them how to be better? Go in and say, "Hi! Good morning," and proudly and confidently introduce yourself and welcome them to your party.

Who is hosting a better party during this video shoot?

On camera, it's your party, too! You are presumably filming something you want people to watch. So, just like at your party – because you want people to come (and stay!) – you roll out the red carpet to make *them* feel good and loved. You have to do the same thing when engaging people whether that's on-camera or in front of a room. You are welcoming them into your sphere of influence so they'll stay long enough to hear why you've asked them into your life. I hope this resonates with you. It's a trick you can use any time of the day, no matter what you are doing. You can make people want to be around you and to listen to you, whether you are at the grocery store, convincing your kids to eat their broccoli, or luring your spouse into helping you clean the kitchen! (Note: When engaging with people in person, remember that a huge way to host the party is to ask them questions and be genuinely interested in them. That makes them feel welcome and wanted by you which makes you someone they want to be around.)

Hosting the party is now part of my job description – my *life* description. I constantly go into audition rooms where I have to convince strangers I am the actor who can best capture a character. These decision makers are often a group of people who are tired, bored, stressed that no actor will fulfill a role, and/or they've got a million other things they are working on for the movie. They are often on their computer or phone and heavily distracted. Needless to say, the vibe that greets me can be extremely unwelcoming and it's my job to relieve *them* of having to host the party in that room. Once I started hosting the party in audition rooms, things shifted dramatically (pun fully intended!).

David Speaks!

I use Kate's host the party tip all the time in my software consulting practice – particularly when I am running meetings or giving presentations. By the way – a meeting should be viewed as a presentation. These meetings are mostly held in a client's conference room. I make sure to take the head of the table no matter who is in the meeting – hey, it's MY party! I'm also sure to meet people as they come into the (MY) room. Always with Kate's voice in my head. Host the party. Host the party.

I purposely up my energy as I know this is my Achilles heel. I don't become fake or try to be somebody I'm not. I just act in my normal way but with an intentional addition of two things: One, I host my party, and two, I increase and sustain my energy. Host the party is the most substantial tip I think I have ever received in business.

Once you put this into practice, you will begin noticing how many people DON'T host the party. Kate has counselled all of my software employees on 'party'. The ones who have a monster desire to grow have embraced the technique have said how much more enjoyable and stress-free running their meetings has become. It is an amazing mental trick that can be used in all aspects of your life.

Chapter 22
They Don't Know That You Don't Know

By Kate Zenna

This chapter is for anyone who has ever found themselves in the midst of a presentation in front of a full room of people when, suddenly, their mind has gone blank. "Brain go bye-bye", as I say!

When you can't remember what you are supposed to say next. When you are so completely nervous about the presentation that something has snuck into your head and pressed PAUSE on your brain. *That* is when you need to remember this super powerful tip: When they are looking at you frozen and mute, they don't know that you don't know what to say! They don't know that you are frozen. They don't know that you are panicking. Unless of course you decide you need to alert the whole world by putting on your best panic face! Worried eyes, sweat forming on your brow, quivering lip. If you can opt for another facial expression option, I would suggest the *Sullivan Nod.*

Years ago, while waitressing at a corporate pub-style restaurant in Toronto, we were forced to watch some training videos created by the lovely folks from HQ. (Yes, I wish *they* had hired ZennaWolfe to help them direct these horrifically boring videos) One of the videos talked about what they called 'The Sullivan Nod'. Not sure why it's called that...one of life's lovely mysteries. Anyway, the Sullivan Nod was suggested to be employed whenever you are talking with your customers. It's a continuous head nod accompanied by a bright smile as you are talking. So if you ask a customer, "Would you like any coffee or dessert?" you should be nodding encouragingly and smiling.

The thinking is that the customer will subconsciously want to imitate your movements and will be more likely to agree and say, "Well, sure. We'll have some coffee and dessert." As a long-time server, I know the increased value in my tips if I could get every customer to order another $10-$15 of food. So, I became a Sullivan Nod devotee. (Aside: Yes, if you do the opposite – shake your head no, furrow your brow, and wince as you offer coffee – you'll be able to cut loose from your shift early because NO ONE will order dessert from a frowning head shaker!) This is a fun thing to try outside of work with friends or family. Many parents already do this when coaxing young children to eat broccoli and peas – keep watch for it!

Kate on set explaining the Sullivan Nod

If you can get The Sullivan Nod firmly implanted as a go-to rescue buoy when you are drowning in the sea, you will find respite long enough to get your thoughts together. The Sullivan Nod forces you to smile and nod. Your brain will follow what your body is doing and become more friendly to you once it's convinced it's out of death's reach. This happy nodding makes your brain feel that everything is okay – you're not in danger of being impaled by a bow and arrow, you're not being chased by a leopard, and these people in front of you are in awe of how you can command a moment with such grace. Show *them* how to pause and take your time like a pro!

What you need to do when that brain takes a brief recess is to take a breath and look at your audience and let them take a good long look at you. Give them the Sullivan Nod. And if you still need more time to get back on track, put it on them. Ask them a question. "How is this sinking in with all of you? It's a lot of information, right? Do you think you can handle it?" You are in front of people for more reasons than to simply make a presentation on some obscure angle of your business or industry. You are also there as a human being to connect with other people. Remember that and connect!

Lesson: There are NO MISTAKES.

Apply this to being on camera. Let's say you are using cue cards or a teleprompter. Let's also say you are speaking directly to the camera and you freeze up. You lose yourself in the cue cards. Here's the pro tip: You look off camera directly at the cue card and start reading it in your head if you need to. You keep yourself smiling and do a small Sullivan Nod. It's actually a very natural look. When people are talking, they don't just look each in the eye the entire time. That can be a bit creepy...

Look off camera a bit. Smile, breathe, pause. Gather yourself and maybe even keep talking. It's fine to look off, to

Chapter 23
Take the Pause!

By Kate Zenna

Perhaps the number one challenge shared by all our clients is their habit of rushing through their speech when they are being filmed. I think they figure the pain will decrease if they finish faster – but it's the pain of watching a less-than-stellar performance that comes next!

Whether that rush is detectable and hidden by a cacophony of 'um' or 'you know' or 'right' or 'like'– it's an element that doesn't serve you the way you think it does. What I've noticed after years of coaching is that so often we are afraid we will be interrupted in conversation and, in turn, we devise ways to impede others from nudging in on our verbal contributions. We all need to think about what we are going to say next and that thinking time is often covered by some word or sound to keep momentum going.

I have seen profound improvements within minutes when I have people slow down by taking intentionally long pauses between words and sentences. Chances are, if you are on stage or on-camera presenting on a topic, no one is going to interrupt you so there's no need to rush and fill every gap to make sure that an audience knows you still have the conch.

This is something that can be practiced every day out in the world with friends and colleagues. You can slow yourself down by finding other ways to let people know you are still speaking despite taking a pause. If your mouth was full of food, for example, you may use your hand to gesture for your friend to wait a moment while you finish chewing so that you can respond to them. They will most likely politely wait. You can then chew and take that time to think about what you really want to say without having someone else enter a new thought into the conversation. You can graduate to trying this without food and eventually feel comfortable enough to use subtle body language to indicate you are still contemplating and sharing. You become a more commanding person in general, but often it takes practice.

Pauses on-camera or during a speech are so powerful. Audiences are *drawn in* for many reasons. They want to hear more from this powerful person who has the strength of character to just stand in front of others and let them behold her/him. They want to know what the heck you're thinking about so they'll wait to hear more. Often we wait until we are well into our last years or decades of life to enjoy the power of the pause. Think of grandparents who take their time to express their words. Or movie stars like Christopher Walken whose pauses are so delicious to watch. You never know what he's going to do or say next, but one thing's for sure, you're riveted!

The ability to have fun with 'the Pause' will allow any opportunities to speak in front of others to be truly enjoyable for you as well as your audience. If you can trust that, while you are struggling in the cold, barren silence of a pause, your audience is being allowed to breathe and take in your very being, you'll be far ahead of the game.

David Speaks!

Since starting ZennaWolfe with Kate and being the beneficiary of coaching from many of our actor-coaches, I have found that I watch TV and movies differently. I now watch knowing there is a complete film crew around them along with a ton of distractions. I marvel at the skills of actors. (And that includes Kate who is a delicious actor – watch her scene at the end of the movie "Chicago" where she doesn't have a single line but commands the screen with her brief performance. Also notice how massive the set and crew and background actors was while she was performing – talk about needing to focus!)

But the thing I watch the most are the pauses. The best actors are so in-the-zone and comfortable that they don't rush anything. The more they pause the more you feel compelled to watch them. It is VERY powerful. As a result of this practice, I now find that I will pause on-purpose and look at my audience when I am speaking just to create more interest in me and what I am saying. This is the complete and 100% opposite of giving a PowerPoint presentation where the star of the presentation are the graphics and words being presented on the screen. I have used PowerPoint only one time in my 35-year working career and it was with a professional gun to my head. It was a speaking engagement in a large auditorium for the employees of the second largest pension fund in the world. It didn't go well and I swore never to share the stage with a software product ever again. I can also promise you this: All of this pausing is going to feel odd at first, but stick with it and use some of Kate's tips that she listed above.

I'll end with this: Own your power. Don't rush. Pause with confidence.

Chapter 24
Perfection Is in the Imperfection

By Kate Zenna

Here's something to wrap your brain around: Being perfect is NOT being perfect.

I have a lot of clients who come to us for coaching. One situation I see over and over again is my client wanting to get it right in the first few takes. That the words are going to be said exactly the way they think they think the words should be said. But there are accidents…

What I teach them is to just keep going – to not 'cut' or stop when a mistake happens. Little imperfections (whether it's not saying the exact words on the script or cue card or you don't know what you are going to say next) are okay because we are human beings. You're allowed to be human. Your mistakes actually make people more comfortable because you are showing yourself as you truly are. Who wants to be with somebody who is perfect? Boring!

You are putting videos up online to connect with your audience. The whole purpose of that is to make yourself endearing and to come across as a real human being so they can feel like you are somebody they can relate to. Big hint: They are not perfect either. They don't want to go to a perfect dentist, doctor, or lawyer. They want to go to a person who is really, really good at what they do. They want to be able to relate to you. And the one thing that all of us can relate to is the fact that none of us are perfect.

Oh, and by the way, we're working with video and we can cut around the bits that don't work. So relax, get messy, be real, and trust that you will be fabulous.

◊ ◊ ◊ ◊ ◊ ◊ ◊ ◊ ◊

David Speaks!

I wish I would have known about this whole perfection thing back when Maggie and I were making the Taliban videos. I didn't know it then, but trying to be perfect was my major problem. I was trying to have a perfect take and, in the process, became a stiff, wooden person who had little resemblance to the person I really am. Now when I am doing my camera work, I know that I might flub. Big deal. I come across better if I correct myself or forget what I'm going to say. It happens all the time when I'm talking to people in real life. I don't ask for a do-over. I just correct myself or remember what I'm going to say and then move on. It doesn't seem to be a problem. It took Kate's coaching, and some intentional work on my part, to get over this whole perfection thing. Once this beast is slayed, it makes being on camera fun with little or no stress.

Try it, you'll like it. And people watching will like it. I promise.

Chapter 25
Think of all the Unflattering Things

By Kate Zenna

Remember the episode of *The Brady Bunch* when Mr. Brady was teaching Greg Brady how to drive? Greg was very nervous about the whole exam and Mr. Brady said something like, "Just imagine the examiner in his underwear, it will take the edge off your nerves."

I recognized *early on* that when I stood up in front of people that I would get really nervous. Really, *really* nervous. I started to notice that I had a running dialogue, actually a monologue, going on in my head. I was making up critical thoughts that the audience was having about me. "She's SO tall." "She should stand up straight." "She thinks she's so great." I realized that this was crazy. People can't be thinking all of these horrible things about me, and if they are – well too bad for them…

When I work with my clients, I try to determine if this dynamic is going on with them. If so, we dig in and find out what that running monologue is and we adjust and just change the tapes. We find ten things the audience would be saying about you if they were you mother…or somebody proud of you. I drill that into my clients' heads so it becomes second nature. I did it with David and his formerly-annoying facial tic discussed in Chapter 7. I told him that he is actually better on camera than me, a professional actor, because he is used to being *himself* and I am used to playing a character or a role. (This is a commonly-shared trait among many professional actors who are often, ironically, very shy people!)

The goal here is to come out and feel that the audience is a warm, supportive group who wants you to succeed and who likes you just the way you are. It should feel like a warm embrace. At first it may feel a little odd, but soon it will be natural. And you'll get to enjoy the benefits of this in all aspects of your life.

Chapter 26
Roll With It

By Kate Zenna

Lean in. Closer. Here's some inside Hollywood scoop: *everybody* flubs lines. Forgets their lines. Has senior moments… So why should you be any different? What we professionals do well is just roll with it. And often we have tons of fun with these flubs. Have you ever watched outtakes from a movie? Pretty hilarious, right? That fun is the gold.

If you are in front of the camera and feel like you are teetering on a balance beam, just keep going. Don't let a little accident or misstep make you fall off your beam. There are no rules here and we have already discussed and agreed to the fact that the perfection is in the imperfection. Oh, and that you can edit the flubs out!

Thinking that you can go through something with absolute precision is ridiculous. It's not human. It's not real. And nobody can relate to you if you try. When you make a mistake, misstep, or wobble – yay! Whether you are in a presentation, a meeting, on stage, or in front of a camera – just go with it (use it!). Always remember that you are in front of people to teach something. You are being an example of a brave person who is getting out there and putting it all on the line. Standing up there – growing and moving your life forward.

Be an example. Show people how to roll with it. They'll love you for it even though they may not realize why!

Part V
A Day in the Studio

"Be not the slave of your own past – plunge into the sublime seas, dive deep, and swim far, so you shall come back with new self-respect, with new power, and with an advanced experience that shall explain and overlook the old."

Ralph Waldo Emerson

Chapter 27
Home, Office, or Studio?

By David Wolfe

We are asked quite often, "Where is the best place to shoot a video?" From the house, the office, or a professional studio – I have quite bit of experience with this having done all three. Here is the good, the bad, and the ugly.

Shooting a video from your home is certainly the easiest place to do it. Roll out of bed, take a shower, set up camera – then it's go time. With the video capabilities of today's tablets and smartphones, you can make some really high-quality videos. Kate uses her home office to submit taped auditions and create internal ZennaWolfe videos with an iPad™ on a small tripod. But what you can't do from home is control your environment. Here is a list of annoyances I have dealt with over the years:

- Family interruptions
- Dog barking
- Phone ringing
- Doorbell ringing
- Text sounds
- The demon people next door
- Air conditioning turning on and off
- Garage door opening
- Creaky floors
- Changing lighting throughout the day
- Bad sound from wireless mic

- Garbage truck beep, beep, beep
- Mailman putting mail in the box
- Airplanes! Freaking airplanes!

And my biggest pet peeve: The dreaded weed eater sounding like a swarm of hornets.

You get the picture. It may not seem like much, but if you are already struggling with getting in front of the camera, then the slightest little thing will throw you off your game. I got to the point where I expected things to go wrong. You can imagine how this came across on camera. (When Kate first looked at some of my old videos she said "You look so pissed off!" My answer: I was. Partially due to the above list and partially due to other variables. See the interview with my daughter Maggie in Chapter 8.) Personally, for me as a sometimes-still novice, I won't do a video at home anymore unless I know it is going to be quick or if it is just an internal communication (sometimes I will send Kate a video email rather than type out a whole long thing), or if I KNOW I can control my environment. Otherwise, I know I am going to be distracted and my performance will suffer in a profound way.

So how about the office? That could work, right? It can, but it can also be a bit like filming from your home. You are exchanging one set of problems and interruptions for another. I've always been 'the boss' but that still hasn't stopped the following from happening:

- Employee interruptions
- Phone ringing
- Email alerts
- Visitors coming in the front door

- HVAC turning on and off
- Sterile environment
- Hearing the people in the suite next door
- The people in the suite next door listening to me record (and commenting!)
- Cleaning crew coming in

Does this hot seat have your name on it?

I still do videos at the office, but they are the same variety as the home-based videos. The problem for home and office-based recording is that you can't control your environment and it's tough to be 'up'! And, usually you are having to do everything yourself AND be 'the talent'. I've seen Kate pull it off but she is a seasoned actor and has pretty much zero problem being in front of the camera. (However, I have been behind the camera with her at her home when she was taping an audition when one of her 87 dogs erupted in barking killing a good take – that's a Kate you don't see every day! Try reminding her to 'host the party' after that!)

For seven years I made all of my videos either from my home or from my office. That was until I met Kate Zenna and she introduced me to the concept of The Studio. I'll start with my conclusion and it's this: I will never, ever do any sort of important video work outside of a professional studio. Period. End of story.

Here is what happens when you go to a good studio to do your video work. First of all, let's think about what is going on. You are driving to the studio in your own car with the express intention of doing one thing – to work on your presentation skills and to make some video magic. No other calls. No employees. No bosses. No weed eaters. Just you, the camera, your coach, and the crew. You are 'the talent'. Every single person there has one mission: make YOU look as good as you can on camera. Right out of the box, this is profoundly different than the home and office options above. When you are doing video work at home or the office, you are trying to fit that activity in. In the studio, that IS the activity. One. Uno.

Chapter 28
Preparation

By David Wolfe

Fun in the studio

When contacted by prospective clients I am always asked at some point, "What's it like going into the studio for the first time?" Well, I was once one of you. I can't say I found it daunting. I think more than anything, as a business owner, I didn't even know how to get started. I wasn't dumb or afraid. I was just ignorant to the process.

Now that I am on the other side of all this, here is the biggest secret about being in the studio: Everything is done for you. The only thing you need to think about is the outcome – what you are trying to accomplish with your film/video project. From there you hire experts – a director, a sound tech, a videographer, and an editor to piece the footage into something that is magic. Sometimes your editor, videographer, and sound tech are the same person.

When you work in the studio, you will get quiet, no interruptions, the ability to completely focus, and have a laboratory within which you can create your vision. These studios are set up to do everything you want. Adjustments can be made on the fly. The crews are used to people like you being on the set. I have always found them incredibly kind to the client sitting in the hot seat.

Which brings me to preparation. What should you be doing in advance of your studio time to get ready? Here are some suggestions:

Visualize having fun. It's going to be fun. As opposed to going into the session with dread and fear, come in looking forward to the new experience. When you are getting ready to go on vacation do you dread that? Answer: You are looking forward to it. Pretend you are going on vacation or, at a minimum, on a field trip.

Visualize having terrific videos. Go out to our website and look at some of the video business cards. That is what YOU will be getting. How cool is that?

Go watch the ZennaWolfe movie at www.zennawolfe.com. That will give you an idea and feel of the energy of a movie film set. This will help set your expectations.

Reread this book. Or at least skim it.

Visualize flubs. That's right – visualize messing up. It's going to happen. So imagine yourself having fun with the flubs and laughing at yourself. Give yourself permission to not be perfect. Know that we are going to be right there with you. Safe hands will be there ready to catch you when you fall.

Briefly look at your answers to the questions you submitted to us. Know that we have the answers to the submitted questions in our hands on the other side of the camera. It is natural to forget some of the answers. We'll help you through that and be your memory.

Be on time. The chances are good there will be a client coming right in behind you. If you are late, then it just cuts into your time. And being late will probably stress you out more than anything else. Leave early from your home or hotel and give yourself plenty of time.

Put yourself in our hands. This is what we do and every single person on the crew is trained to focus on you and to ensure you come across well on camera. We focus on making sure that process, from start to finish, is comfortable and memorable.

ZennaLude™

PREPARATION TIPS FOR A GREAT TIME IN THE STUDIO.

Get Your Breath On!

Before clients come in to the studio to shoot we give them a list of preparation tips. The top of this list is PRACTICE INTENTIONAL BREATHING. It's a really simple and effective exercise. What I suggest is that a few times a day, you take the time to breathe in deeply, very slowly, hold your breath for a moment and then exhale very slowly. If you do a few sets of five to seven repetitions of breath, you'll get practiced at something that will come in very handy on set when the nerves are keeping you and your friend Oxygen from joining your party!

I was working with a client recently who would take a deep breath in and then exhale right before he would begin to speak on-camera. Luckily, I caught it early and we were able to make a fabulous and very simple adjustment. Rather than exhaling, I got him to <u>hold</u> his breath deep into his belly as he began to speak on camera. It meant his stomach had to be slightly engaged to keep the air in there and it also led to him having much greater clarity in his voice and his presence, not to mention it's great posture support. It made him sound more authoritative and confident. Because he had practiced this intentional breathing prior to coming in to work with me, he was easily able to bring that into his performance. We were back to work quickly and it was smooth sailing from then on. Try it. Just writing this and telling you about reminds me that I could use a few of these, too.

As you slowly count to seven in your head, take in a slow, deep breath. Deep into your lungs and belly.

Hold your inhale in for seven seconds.

SLOWLY, for a count of seven, exhale gently.

Repeat this a few times during the day in sets of five breaths. This is a great thing to do in traffic, in an elevator, in line for lunch...

Careful – doing this in the afternoon may perk you up naturally so you may not need that afternoon coffee!

Get Your Walk On!
See if you can find time to take a 20-30 minute walk every day. If you already do this daily, then try adding an extra walk to your regime. Prepping for your shoot is part of the fun. You'll have time to think about what you want to get out of your videos and visualize having fun. Think of your clients, your family, and all the people who will benefit from the increase in business and connection that a great video will offer.

Get Your Muscle On!

I love to randomly jump out of my desk chair and do ten pushups or twenty-five sit ups or twenty jumping jacks – especially when I'm feeling super lazy. Sometimes I'll put on some silly dance music and dance for one minute and go back to work. If you practice this random play a week or so before you come into the studio, you'll be more primed to play and have fun in front of the camera. It gets your blood and spirit flowing and that's exactly what you want in the studio!

Get Your Laugh On!

There are countless research studies declaring the health benefits of laughing. But for most of us, it's a tough thing to do without the help of someone else. In privacy, take a minute and just start laughing. You can pretend you're on a phone call with someone who is telling you the most hilarious story. If you're in front of your computer, you can pretend you are reading or watching something funny. If you have a book and a park bench nearby, you can sit there and pretend to be reading something hilarious and no one will think you're crazy! OR you can just start laughing wherever and for no reason. Once you get going, you may just keep going! It's so much fun and it will get you out of your comfort zone and remind you that you have control over your mood and perspective. It's especially great if you're having a challenging day. **NOTE: If you are challenged to find a private place to do this, try your car on your way to work or in the bathroom while pretending to be on a call.

Being able to easily and quickly get a big genuine smile on your face will help SO much as you are filming your videos. It can make all the difference if you begin speaking from this emotional place. It's how you greet people at your party, right?

Chapter 29
What You Can Expect
During Your Studio Session

By David Wolfe

You can expect to be <u>surprised</u> at the support will you receive from the crew and from the actor-coaches. You will be surprised at the lifelong tools you will be given – tools that will be benefit you for the rest of your life. You will be surprised at how much fun you have in studio and at how often you laugh and how cool it feels to be the STAR.

You can expect to have <u>regrets</u>. That you didn't do this sooner. You will have regrets that the session has to end. We see this again and again – our clients don't want the session to end. They're in a groove and they have the whole camera thing figured out. You will have regrets that others, your friends and peers, don't have the bravery you do. You will want your colleagues to have the same experience that you had.

You can expect to have increased <u>confidence</u>. You will now be able to see yourself in full authenticity, which will show itself in your personal relationships and with customers – whether it be in one-on-one communications, group meetings, presentations or speaking in public. Sure, you may still have some anxiety – Kate and I still do when we have to perform, but you will have tools to get your energy up along with some triggers that we teach. You will also have some insight into how you limited yourself before. You might even slay some dragons like I did with my facial tic.

You can expect to gain <u>experience</u>. You will gain experience in appearing as your genuine self and not some campy version of yourself. Going forward, when you get a business idea that you want to communicate via video, arrange your camera, shoot a couple of takes, pick the best, load that onto your website and be done all in about 45 minutes.

More on-set fun

Chapter 30
Hair and Makeup

By Kate Zenna

Where do I start when it comes to hair and makeup for anyone who wants to be on-camera in a professional capacity? Here's the truth – you need it. Done by a pro. Not your neighbor. Not your niece or nephew. Not your girlfriend (unless she's a pro). And by a 'pro', I mean someone who works often, not once a year, but <u>often</u>, on a film/TV set. This person needs to understand how digital video cameras capture color and texture of skin and makeup. They need to be very used to watching you on-camera through a monitor and up close. They need to be looking at every stray hair in person and then go and check what the camera is picking up because the two are often very different.

I've worked with all kinds of hair and makeup professionals throughout my journey, and when you find a great one, you stay in touch! When you experience a bad one (after it's too late to fix it), you forgive yourself for not asking to see a replay of your takes as you film. For headshots, I once had a makeup artist use a ridiculous amount of powder on my face. But she assured me up and down that, for this photo session, it would be exactly what was needed. Well, none of the photos were useable. None. And it was before digital retouching. This was all on film, so the hours of preparation and shooting was a complete waste. I was too young to question the supposed professional – at the very least I should have gotten a complimentary re-shoot.

I tape at home for many auditions, and for each one, I wish I could justify having a professional hair and makeup artist pop over to help me. The number of times I end up taping a superb take only to realize that a strand of my hair was somehow sticking straight out of my head horizontally – well I can't tell you how many…a lot!

I'm always on the lookout for terrific hair and makeup artists who are wonderful people to work with and talented when it comes to bringing out the best in all faces. Here's how you tell if the makeup artist is great: You aren't ever, for one moment, looking at the makeup on the person. You are focused on their eyes and what they are saying.

Please don't skimp on this. If you are going to create a professional video calling card, make sure you do it right. You're not being egotistical or self-centered to hire a film/TV makeup artist. You are being smart. You are making another very important move toward attracting the clients of your dreams. Remember, there are clients out there looking for YOU. Make sure that when they do get a chance to see you, they're not looking at Groucho Marx or your crazy aunt who still uses blush like it is 1982.

Oh, and yes. Boys need makeup too. Every boy, guy, man!

Chapter 31
The Production Crew: Where for Art Thou?

By Kate Zenna

I want to share some of what we've learned working with production crew professionals. Depending on the size of your shoot, there are people – all of whom must be talented and experienced in things like shooting video, lighting, capturing sound, doing the hair and makeup, and offering production assistance – that you'll need to find. Where do you start?

Oh, your nephew has a camera and your neighbor works at a makeup counter at Bloomingdale's and surely your son can hold a boom mic and, heck, who needs an assistant? Ok. Go for it. Call me next week when you need to re-shoot.

Why do we hire experts – experienced, seasoned, talented and lovely professional film production people? Because you're going to be exceptionally busy doing your job which is to get your message across in an authentic and camera-friendly manner. That's going to (or should!) take up all of your attention. This means that you want to make sure that whoever is in charge of making you look awesome on-camera has 100+ tricks up his/her sleeve to allow YOU to be beautiful. That videographer needs to know creative lighting set ups, his/her camera settings backwards and forwards and have artistry when setting up a shot. It matters. Maybe not for a quick and casual Instagram video, but it matters if this is the one video you and your referrers have as a tool to share what you do professionally.

With all of our shoots, regardless of size, we only work with seasoned and talented production experts. Our team of pros knows what it takes to be a ZennaWolfe crew member. They, as we all do, have 100% focus on the client. Our sets are not ones where egos flail all over the place. Sure, you may learn that the person behind the camera at your Video Business Card shoot just finished shooting an independent feature starring your favorite TV actor, but today, that videographer/cinematographer is here to make YOU shine.

We find most of our production team members through referrals – talented and <u>pleasant</u> people often hang in groups. Our crew members are busy professionals and fly in and out of ZennaWolfe shoots when they are not on a film/TV set. They have incredible talent and know how to work quickly. We give them the freedom to work with us while they are pursuing their career in Hollywood. Same is true for our actor-coaches.

We do everything we can to extract the very best performance for our clients and we do the same for our crew members. It's all hands on deck and all fun and focus in the ZW Studio.

Kate reminding David who the CEO of ZennaWolfe really is...

Chapter 32
Sound

By Kate Zenna

For the most part, while on set, you will be wearing a portable mic called a 'lav'. The sound man will weave the wires through your shirt and you will be given a little control unit to put in your pocket or have clipped to your shirt. When David used to do his videos on his own, he would skip having a microphone and it sounded like he was talking from inside a tunnel. He did switch over to a wireless mic at some point and it sounded much better; although, more often than not, he would get a hiss during playing mainly because he had no idea what he was doing. He's a software guy, remember?

After the sound tech gets your microphone attached, you will get a sound check. Sometimes adjustments need to be made. There is a chance that you will not have a lav mic but rather a boom mic will be employed. That's ok, especially if you are in a quiet studio; although, we prefer the lav mics. You've probably seen these boom microphones on TV shows or in movies because occasionally they will be seen dipping into your TV picture. Even though you won't have the mic on your shirt the sound, if managed by a professional sound engineer, will come across just fine.

Warning: When you are wearing a lav mic, you need to watch what you say after they call CUT (and you head to the restroom)! Everything you say will be heard and captured until you power off or mute your control unit…

Chapter 33
Sitting in the Hot Seat

By David Wolfe

Kate's turn in the hot seat

There you are sitting in 'the chair'. Holy cow – look at all those lights and cameras! And who are all these people who are staring at *me*. Now is the time when you will completely forget what you are going to say. Brain lock. Freeze.

Welcome to The Club. It happens to all of us. And in talking to the actors we employ at ZennaWolfe, it happens to them too. The difference is in how they handle it. Kate was on a TV series a few years ago and, while she was going through the audition process, she completely flubbed the line; however, she handled the misstep so well that it was the differentiator in getting the role. This may not happen to you, but if it does, there are different ways to get over it. One is, in advance, begin the visualization process of sitting in the studio. If you can't do that then go to the ZennaWolfe website (www.zennawolfe.com).

We have lots of studio pictures. Many of them are of me sitting in THAT chair.

The second thing you can do is to simply be rational. You are not going to die as a result of your terrific day in the studio. Think about all the difficult things you have already accomplished in your life. For most things, the before is much worse than the after.

Three – why are you doing the video? The camera is just a piece of plastic. Here's a secret: Most of what gets shot ends up on the editor's floor. Everybody flubs lines. Everybody. Go watch the blooper reels that run at the end of some movies. We are just looking for the inspirational gold that *will* occur during your shoot. Nobody is judging you while you sit in the hot seat. And with that, here's another bit of insider knowledge: Crew members who are working behind the camera HATE being in front of the camera. You will have all their support and considerable talents to help you shine. And will you will have their admiration and respect for being so brave and cool.

Chapter 34
You Know What You Are Talking About

By David Wolfe

What sort of aids or cheat sheets should you use for your day in the studio? You don't have to have any for a variety of reasons, but let's go ahead and walk through some options for your consideration. Some people just make it up as they go. There are just a few folks who are good at this. Most aren't and fill their dialogue with a lot of 'umms' and 'you-knows'. You also run the risk of looking shifty because you are trying to figure out what you are going to say next. If you get good at 'taking the pause' (see Chapter 23) then this may be the easiest way to go.

One option is to memorize your script. There is a fair bit of work involved with this. If you are not an actor, then memorization is likely a muscle that is not exercised much. You may come across as inauthentic because you are trying to remember your lines. I did this for years and frankly didn't do it very well. I also found it stressful particularly when I had shot a two-minute video perfectly and then botched the last sentence because I relaxed mentally. Very debilitating to have to shoot the whole video over again. Cue cards can also work, but many times you can see the eyes reading left to right. This takes practice and is not natural for us common folk. Cards have to be created, you need a second person to handle, and you have to be in sync with them.

Another option is using a teleprompter. I have a lot of experience using them and, under the right circumstances, a teleprompter <u>can</u> work. Like memorizing, this is a muscle that is rarely used. I had to develop the skill and have probably stood in front of a teleprompter about thirty anguishing hours. It usually takes time to sync the speed of the teleprompter to your speaking delivery. I've had it too slow and too fast. Usually takes four to five reads to get the machine in sync with your talking speed. Using the teleprompter also adds one more variable to what can go wrong. A couple of times when I was trying to do all of this on my own at my office, I just had to shut it down for the day because the teleprompter software broke down. We had a client at ZennaWolfe who insisted on using a teleprompter and everything went fine because we hired a teleprompter specialist to be in studio with us. However, Teleprompters tend to make you look wooden because you're not putting any emotion into it. Your eyes may look shifty because you are reading left-to-right and they can be twinkle-less because you are so focused on reading and staying in concert with the machine.

When Kate and I were shooting the ZennaWolfe promotional movie, I was in the hot seat first. Australian actor Shane Connor was going to help me through the session. While everything was getting set up, I felt a pair of eyes on me. Shane was watching me as I reviewed some notes from my cheat sheet. I could tell he wasn't pleased with me. Big Shane Scowl. Finally, we got started and I did my first take, which pretty much sucked. Shane walked over to me and in his best Crocodile Dundee accent said, "What you have their mate?", referring to the talking points I was holding in my hand. I told him they were my notes. He asked to see them so I handed him the sheets. He proceeded to tear them up right in front of me with this admonition that I think I will carry with me the rest of my life: "You don't need these – you know what you are talking about." And you know what – he was right! I *did* know what I was talking about (which in this case was ME) and the rest of the session with Shane was terrific as was my Video Business Card that is on our website.

David on set with actor Shane Connor. Notice that David no longer has his notes in his hands...

And with that bit of information, Kate and I changed our interview and filming tactics. Since then, we ask our clients to send us questions <u>and</u> the answers to the questions in advance of the shoot. Our direction involves asking the client questions off-camera. What appears on camera is the answer to the posed question. No need for memorization, cue cards, teleprompters, or notes *because they know what they are talking about* and are simply answering questions. Time and time again we have observed our clients forgetting about the cameras because they are simply engaged in a conversation with a ZennaWolfe actor-coach. This approach allows our clients to know what is coming because they supplied the question and the answer to us. This dynamic keeps them from doing the psycho stare into the camera and they come across more naturally because, well, they are being themselves and just having a conversation. There just

Chapter 35
Transformation

By David Wolfe

You are undoubtedly familiar with *The Ugly Duckling* by Hans Christian Andersen. This is the story about a homely little bird born in a barnyard who suffers abuse from the others around him until, much to his delight (and to the surprise of others), he matures into a beautiful swan, the most beautiful bird of all.

You may experience the same thing during your studio day. You walk in 'ugly' and you leave beautiful in every way – emotionally, physically, psychologically, and professionally. It is a day of self-actualization and pride – most people don't have the bravery to walk through the mirror of fear. You will NEVER be afraid of speaking or being on camera again. Some minor flutters of anxiety, sure. But fear? Nope.

You will find yourself becoming more aggressive with your marketing because you have added a major weapon into your tool kit. You now know how to appear 'up' on camera. Our coaches find your Achilles heel (mine is that my energy wanes the longer I am on camera) and give you techniques on how to combat your humanness AFTER you leave the studio so that you rock it the next time you have to give a presentation or want to command attention.

Your self-esteem is going to blip up. You've slain the beast and you have these awesome videos to show for it. Expect for some people to be a little jealous because you've done what they, maybe, are afraid to do. I can promise you that if/when that happens you will be ready for any well-meaning 'friends' who try to rain on your parade. You will smile and nod (The Sullivan Nod!) and not care a bit. You have crossed the field and are now playing for the other team.

You will soon find yourself watching actors on TV differently. YOU have been in front of a camera now and a whole new world has opened up. How much the really good actors pause (particularly Mark Ruffalo!). Watch how they *own* the camera.

David shining. Thank you Shane!

The next time you are at a party and people are taking pictures, you will no longer try and hide. And you'll no longer look directly at the camera either because you have gotten used to people all around you in the studio shooting shots of you. And speaking of parties – you will begin to develop the habit of hosting a party everywhere you go. (And a quick aside on party hosting. Kate and I are *very* different people. How she and I host our respective parties is different. She is more 'up' and, well, *hostess-y*. When I host, I am more parental and authoritative. In a business setting, I am hosting <u>that</u> party. It means I will make you want to be on time and know that I am in complete control and command. With both of us – all eyes are on us because we are the center of that particular universe.)

You will soon be known. Several times over the last month, I met new people at a client site in San Diego. When I introduced myself, they said, "I know. I've watched your videos."

Sweet.

Part VI
The Building of a Company
(Quite by accident…)

"Hitch your wagon to a star."

Ralph Waldo Emerson

We have been publishing the newsletter "Host the Party" for the past two years. It is a mostly-monthly publication that we send to our client, prospects, studio crew, and other business associates. When we started creating it, we had no idea how many emails and letters we would get from our readers.

So, here for your reading pleasure, are some newsletter articles that talk about how we met and formed our company.

Enjoy!

Kate Zenna
David Wolfe

Studio City, California
September 20, 2016

Chapter 36
A Chance Meeting

By Kate Zenna and David Wolfe

In the past year, the question both of us have been asked more than any other question is: "How did you two meet?" Our answer: "Well – we actually met online. And no, it was not a dating site..."

David: In April 2014 I was reading Arianna Huffington's book *Thrive: The Third Metric to Redefining Success and Create a Life of Well-Being, Wisdom, and Wonder*. She likens our drive for money and power to two legs of a three-legged stool. They may hold us up temporarily, but sooner or later we're going to topple over. We need a third leg – a third metric for defining success – to truly thrive. That third metric, she writes, includes our well-being, our ability to draw on our intuition and inner wisdom, our sense of wonder, and our capacity for compassion and giving.

It was the giving part that really got me thinking. I had achieved some success in business – had some money and power but I was failing on the giving side. I wasn't really interested in coaching Little League or serving in a food kitchen. But I did like the idea of working with people who were willing to 'raise their hand' and to create their own business ventures. That was something I could have passion about. At the back of Thrive there was an appendix which listed out various organizations where somebody could volunteer.

The one that caught my eye was MicroMentor.

Kate: Not long before I met David, I had been cast as the lead in a hot new family drama TV series pilot. When the pilot wasn't given the greenlight, I was back in the pool of auditioning actors and knew that my big break may have come just come and gone – never to return. So I began to develop a business around a food product I had created – I've always been an avid amateur chef. I had come to a point in my pursuit of this food venture where I knew I was stuck. I knew my acting career was precarious at best and, if I wanted to find stable success, I needed to take action and create a side business.

The problem was I had taken the food thing as far as I could and needed sound advice regarding my next steps. I didn't want to take on an equity partner because I knew from recent experience the treachery of that path and I didn't have money to spend on accountants and lawyers to get the answers I needed. What I needed was a 'Finance and Accounting Mentor' – someone with whom I could talk things through and benefit from their business experience. One day, in a fit of my trademark haste and exasperation, I simply Googled 'Finance and Accounting Mentor'. Up popped MicroMentor.org. I perused the site and took a huge leap of faith and posted a very vague, yet apparently well-written, plea for help.

David: So I went to their website and I signed up. Said I would be willing to help in accounting/finance and marketing. For the most part, I was completely underwhelmed with the 'entrepreneurs' that were listed on the site. I was seeing a lot of comments (and I am not making this up) like: "I don't know what I would like to do. I need somebody to tell me…" or "This seems better than trying to get a job…"

So much for me giving back…I was completely turned off. I turned off all email notifications and went back to my old two-legged-stool life. For reasons unknown, I returned (more accurately, I was pulled back) to the MicroMentor website the last week of June. With the click of a mouse, my life was changed. There was a posting from a woman named Kate. It seems she wanted some advice around how to structure her food company start-up.

Kate: After I posted my plea for help on MicroMentor, I looked through the people who had signed on as Mentors. I think I sent messages to three or four of them. I wasn't impressed by the other people who posted, but I set my ego aside and waited patiently for someone to respond. Within a day or two of my postings I received notice that a man named David Wolfe had accepted my request for mentorship and, "would I like to connect with David Wolfe regarding my need for a Finance and Accounting Mentor?" I clicked whatever button would get me started on a call. I sent a message to this David Wolfe man and kept things very vague. I was nervous about someone stealing my food venture idea. I was also concerned about meeting a strange man online so I didn't share details about my acting work or personal life. I went and Googled this David Wolfe to see who he could be.

David: We connected on the website on July 2nd and scheduled an introductory call for the next day. Before the meeting, I realized I wasn't that current on the things Kate wanted to talk about. It had been years (decades?) since I had done any research on what the best states to incorporate in were. She also had questions around Sub-S corporations vis-à-vis LLCs. So I sat down and did some research. Even though this was free work, I still want to be prepared for my client meetings

– whether it is for money or for free. I want to give the best service I can. Still do.

Kate: Before we met I began to get really clear on what it was that I wanted mentorship in. I put together materials that may help inform a conversation with my new mentor and I continued to do research on this David Wolfe. I was satisfied that he wasn't wanted for murder and relaxed until our first call happened.

David: I called her and introduced myself. How can I help you?

And then 'the Z' was off...Kate began long, long, long and passionate description of what she was trying to do with her food business. I was taking a lot of notes as she talked – but the one that got a big box around it said:

Force
Powerhouse
She Needs Me

I was very impressed with Kate. She had DRIVE, a willingness to fail, vision, the strength of character to ask for help, and was very open. I liked how she was pushing the ball down the field – not blindly but also not paralyzed by not having it all figured out (starting a company is a very messy endeavor...). And she was smart. Very. Finally (finally!) she stopped talking. I told her my thoughts on her incorporation questions. But I also told her that my real strengths were in marketing and business strategy – and I would be willing to help her in that arena if she was interested. In remembering back, she wasn't that interested in my offer. She was guarded. I now know some of her pre-ZW history and why she was so guarded.

Kate: Our call happened on my way home from Santa Monica after a commercial audition. I remember pulling off Sepulveda Blvd and parking next to a gas station so I wouldn't risk dropping the call on my way over the hill to the Valley in Los Angeles. The call was, I think, at least an hour long. I got a good feeling from David. I had pre-given him a healthy amount of respect for wanting to 'mentor'. I knew I was worthy of an experienced business person's mentorship because I craved learning and was willing to do what they suggested because I'd exhausted all of my amateur business moves to that point.

I also intuitively felt honesty from this man. I wasn't sure if it was because he was a Texan, but part of me felt that could be it. With me being Canadian, there was something familiar about someone who had done a lot of successful business based on a handshake. I understood that well. I was raised by a very down-to-earth and working class British man and a school-teacher mother who taught my brother and me the value of living by your word with a tremendous amount of integrity. In short, to live without guile. I am cut from 'honest cloth'!

David: I was in Los Angeles three weeks later and met with Kate for what was supposed to be a short lunch. It went on for four hours. Terrific meeting. That was on a Monday. That following Saturday, five days later, I called Kate with this idea of having professional working actors coach business professionals, like me, in front of the camera...

Kate: We met in Los Angeles and when he suggested I pick him up from his business meeting and drive together to our lunch meeting spot, I said I'd pay for his Uber. Which I did. I also paid for lunch. Which I've learned was a big check mark to David. Since I was 'receiving' the mentorship, I should be the one expressing gratitude to this person for sharing his knowledge. Obviously, he didn't abduct me. Quite the opposite. I feel that meeting was the first day I became truly unleashed and free. Oh, and yes, because his videos were so bad, it led to me offering to mentor him for free in return because I knew I could make him better on camera in a day. He was such a nice guy in person, there was no reason for him to be scaring people in those videos!

I think the real lessons in this partnership between David and me can be summarized as follows:

- Ask for help
- Listen to those who give you the help you ask for. But discern
- Just put yourself out there
- Listen to your intuition
- Always move forward
- Nothing ventured, nothing gained
- With the proper mix of talents and needs, you can build a sustaining relationship

Or as David says – you can make one plus one equal three.

Chapter 37
Do You Hear the Grasshopper
Which is at Your Feet?

By Kate Zenna and David Wolfe

David: If you are of a certain age then you probably remember the series *Kung Fu*, which starred David Carradine as 'Caine' and aired in the early 1970's. Flashbacks were used to recall specific lessons from Caine's childhood training in the monastery from his teacher, the blind Master Po. From the pilot:

Master Po: Close your eyes. What do you hear?
Young Caine: I hear the water. I hear the birds.
Po: Do you hear your own heartbeat?
Caine: No.
Po: Do you hear the grasshopper which is at your feet?
Caine: Old man, how is it that you hear these things?
Po: Young man, how is it that you do not?

From then on, Caine was always referred to as 'Grasshopper'.

Early in my relationship with Kate (and for a total of about ten days), I was 'Master' David and she was 'Young' Kate. I was the mentor and she was my protégé. During this early process I asked to see her notes and financial analysis on the food venture she was kicking off. She was embarrassed to show me. Afraid that I would comment on her lack of organization and financial acumen. I wrote these words to her in an email that launched our partnership:

"Grasshopper, you had me at LLC."

Three short weeks later we were incorporated, shares were issued, and we were legal partners. Three weeks after that we were in the studio in Dallas filming our first video with me receiving my first of many in-front-of-camera trainings from my talented partner.

Each of us has the identical painting of a grasshopper hanging in our respective offices. Speaking only for myself, it is a daily reminder of how far we have come as business partners but also of the equality in our relationship. That day was when I stopped being her mentor. I eased down and she rose up and we met in the middle and shook hands. Partners.

Kate: I clearly remember the feeling that I had when I read those words in an email from David, "Grasshopper, you had me at LLC." It was the equivalent of reaching a plateau after a long hike up an endless mountain. I didn't realize that I had always been waiting or looking for a business mentor to declare themselves in such a way. I have often sensed that I had big things to offer but was continually snarled up by my creative energies which made it a challenge to focus, see things through and have the confidence to learn all that I needed to learn. I was running on pure instinct and intuition and I knew I needed structure and expertise if I was to execute on any of my 'brilliant' endeavors.

I am a self-declared 'praise-driven' person. I navigated the school system with ease because of this. I will succeed at all costs when I am assured I will receive praise for my efforts along the way. I suspect that acting as a profession was initially appealing because to win praise in this industry is a massive challenge and subsequently, the hugest of accomplishments.

I sensed that I had found not only a 'praiser' in David but also a 'stayer'. Because his innate nature led him to mentor, I gauged that at the very least I knew his *spirit* was in the right place. After all, he had sought out a mentorship organization so that he could offer his guidance to people looking for such guidance.

When I look at my Grasshopper painting, I remember the warmth of that feeling I had when we first decided to partner. We all need mentors. People outside our immediate family who step forward to support our pursuits as best they can – to push us farther along than we would get on our own. Having your talents, skills, goals, spirit and potential recognized by a person outside your immediate family...well, that's a pretty special find.

Chapter 38
Lennon & McCartney and Zenna & Wolfe

By Kate Zenna and David Wolfe

Many people now that John Lennon and Paul McCartney were music partners – that they co-wrote their songs together. This is only partially true. Yes, they were partners, but they actually wrote most of their songs separately with the other partner adding sections or words from time to time. They were, in truth, fairly competitive with each other. The song Yesterday, for example, was written 100% by Paul but it is credited to Lennon-McCartney. By an agreement made before the Beatles became famous, Lennon and McCartney were credited equally with songs that either one of them wrote while their partnership lasted.

David: ZennaWolfe just entered its third year of business. Before we incorporated, and only shortly after we met for the first time face-to-face, Kate and I had a Lennon-McCartney type discussion. Both of us had a lot of business things going on at the time. I had my software consulting company, Lupine Partners that took up a lot of my time while Kate had a host of projects in various stages of development: Film production, commercials, acting jobs, the food business that originally brought us together, and her band, Pointe Claire.

We asked each other: What percentage of our time would each of us spend on ZW versus our separate ventures? Shoulders were shrugged. Who knows? So right out of the box there was inequality. Time-wise one partner would almost always be getting the short end of the stick. Why should Kate work so hard on getting this new baby birthed when David is only working on his software company? Resentment and recriminations were sure to follow closely behind. It could only be unequal. That is when I brought the Lennon-McCartney model to Kate.

Kate: Of course I knew John Lennon and Paul McCartney, but I wasn't aware of their partnership and that for the most part they didn't actually write their songs together. As David was describing the potential problem, I was amazed at how he was ahead of it before it was even a problem. We had literally just met and he was already showing his fairness and vision – qualities I was starved for at the time after my recent business experiences and failed partnerships. We talked about this Lennon-McCartney notion in concept and practicality. And we talked about what would be excluded. We weren't partners yet but the easiness of our conversation and the professional affection and appreciation we had for each other was there from the start. So, I went off and thought about it. I 'wore' it for some days and weeks. I had worked hard on my ventures, I thought – but then so had he and for a longer period of time. I don't know or remember if I ever went back to David and said "I'm in". We just went down a road of sharing and building. A theme of 'we' and 'us' was there from the start with us and I'm sure it was because of this model that David presented to me.

David: I had such high regard for Kate from the very start. She is even better and more talented than I saw from the beginning. Loyal too. This model (which I don't think we ever formally agreed to but has happened nonetheless...) has really freed us up to try things and to brainstorm possibilities because all of it flows through the same ZennaWolfe bank account. No LLCs for each deal or any of that nonsense. Lennon-McCartney only works if 1+1=3. If the union itself adds value. Lennon and McCartney were both better because they were partners. They had the other person pushing them. They had competition, camaraderie, and trust.

Kate and I have this same dynamic in our working life. I don't think ZennaWolfe would have exploded like it has had we not structured the company and our partnership the way we did. Yes, we disagree – but only on priorities and tactics. Never about ownership percentages or money. THAT particular ship sailed long ago after only one conversation.

About ZennaWolfe Media Solutions

ZENNAWOLFE offers on-camera training for people and companies who know the power and value of video in today's marketplace. Our clients are job-seekers, recent college graduates, finance-seeking entrepreneurs, realtors, bankers, medical professionals, and consulting firms large and small who know how critical it is to be well-presented, natural, personable, and compelling when representing their professional interests. What our clients also know, is that 'on-camera' training extends into the boardroom and pitch-sessions, in business meetings and interviews and general management and leadership. No one can know how they come across until they see themselves nervous, uncomfortable, and stressed on-camera.

ZENNAWOLFE ON-CAMERA TRAINING is unique because our trainers are actual, working Hollywood actors. Our **ACTOR-COACHES** are passionate about their own career and also about making each and every **ZENNAWOLFE** client 'shine' their brightest. They have built a career around their learned skills of not only being 'comfortable' in stressful and nerve-wracking situations, but *thriving* in those hot seats. 'Shining your brightest' goes hand-in-hand with being 'authentic' and honestly enthusiastic. Our training offers you tools and techniques to ignite YOUR unique essence. No single coaching session is the same because no single person is the same. The **ZENNAWOLFE ACTOR-COACHES** know this truth intimately; they've made careers out of honing and honoring their star quality.

ZENNAWOLFE ON-CAMERA TRAINING is available for individuals, company staff, and executives and also as an addition to any of our video production services. Contact us to learn more about how we can make YOU and YOUR TEAM shine.

Ready for the Hot Seat?

(More importantly – are you ready to begin YOUR journey to health, wealth, fortune, and fame?)

Here is how you too can work with an amazing ZennaWolfe actor-coach:

Step 1: Email David at dwolfe@zennawolfe.com

Step 2: Talk to Kate and David on the phone about what you want to accomplish.

Step 3: We send you a proposal designed to fit your unique needs and circumstances.

Step 4: You book your time in the studio.

Step 5: You arrive at our studio with a smile on your face, an open heart, and an open mind ready to begin the first day of the rest of your life.

Step 6: You end your time with us armed with more life tools than you ever imagined.

Step 7: For the rest of your life you SHINE!

The ZennaWolfe studio is located in Studio City, California. We are within walking distance to CBS Studios and very short drive to Disney, Warner Brothers, and Universal Studios. Why not make a weekend of it?

Ask us about our Private Executive Coaching and Group Training offerings!

www.zennawolfe.com

9 781634 917377